Soul

100 ESSENTIAL ... THE ROUGH GUIDE

There are more than one hundred and fifty Rough Guide
travel, phrasebook, and music titles, covering destinations
from Amsterdam to Zimbabwe, languages from Czech to
Vietnamese, and musics from World to Opera and Jazz

Other 100 Essential CD titles

Blues • Classical • Country • Opera
Reggae • Rock • World

Rough Guides on the Internet

C11941

Rough Guide Credits

Text editors: Orla Duane, Joe Staines
Series editor: Mark Ellingham
Typesetting: Katie Pringle

Publishing Information

This first edition published October 2000 by
Rough Guides Ltd, 62–70 Shorts Gardens, London WC2H 9AH

Distributed by the Penguin Group:

Penguin Books Ltd, 27 Wrights Lane, London W8 5TZ
Penguin Putnam, Inc., 375 Hudson Street, New York 10014, USA
Penguin Books Australia Ltd, 487 Maroondah Highway,
PO Box 257, Ringwood, Victoria 3134, Australia
Penguin Books Canada Ltd, 10 Alcorn Avenue,
Toronto, Ontario, Canada M4V 1E4
Penguin Books (NZ) Ltd, 182–190 Wairau Road,
Auckland 10, New Zealand

Typeset in Bembo & Helvetica to an original design by Henry Iles
Printed in Spain by Graphy Cems

A catalogue record for this book is available
from the British Library
ISBN 1-85828-562-3

Soul

100 ESSENTIAL CDs THE ROUGH GUIDE

by Peter Shapiro

ROUGH
GUIDES

Contents

781.644 SMA

C11941

Introduction

The **Rough Guide to Essential Soul CDs** isn't merely a list of the hundred greatest soul albums in the world ... ever. Instead, it is a book that encapsulates the entire history of soul music in just 200 pages. Celebrating both the best-selling album in the history of the free world and a compilation of records so obscure that only the musicians' mothers ever owned copies, the *Rough Guide to Essential Soul CDs* traces the music's path, with a brief stopover in Ethiopia, from a rootsy righteousness born in the Pentecostal churches in cotton country to its present-day incarnation as the dream weaver of ghetto fabulous fantasies.

The church of soul music explored here is a broad one, so there's room for Louis Jordan and the Clovers, the Swan Silvertones and the Soul Stirrers, Chic and Teena Marie, Cameo and the Gap Band. There are those who think that housing both Mahalia Jackson (or, even worse, Sylvester) and Otis Redding under the banner of soul music is a heresy but, as this book will hopefully prove, soul has never been about purity. From Nat "King" Cole to Mary J. Blige, all of these artists are indisputably part of the same continuum.

While everyone from 11-year-old prodigies to former folk singers from London get a look-in, this book does not cover certain digressions (house music and Northern soul) from soul's main conversation between its religious roots and its material longings. Nor does it cover either of the crucially distinct genres that bookend it – the blues and hip-hop. However, discussing soul music in the 1990s without engaging with hip-hop is impossible, and artists who span the divide like Missy Elliott and Lauryn Hill are covered as well.

As you'd imagine, narrowing this book down to a hundred CDs was excruciating. In fact, the list wasn't completely settled until just hours before it hit the typesetting machines. This was due not just to indecisiveness, but to the current difficulty in locating far too many great recordings. So, without resorting to ludicrously priced Japanese imports or ten-disc box sets, this is a guide to music that'll make you want to do the popcorn in your underwear in the rain, and to songs that have acted as mediators in countless romances to create a new rhapsodic language.

Acknowledgements

Thanks to everyone at the Rough Guides – particularly my editors Orla Duane, Joe Staines and Jonathan Buckley who put up with my insistence that a six-CD box set was not an unreasonable recommendation (even though they won), Nikky Twyman for proofreading, Katie Pringle for typesetting – Pooh Daddy, YT, Michael Schenker and, most of all, to my wife, Rachael, who once again tolerated my bouts of insomnia more than any reasonable person should have to.

BLACKstreet

Another Level

Interscope, 1996

After Teddy Riley changed the face of R&B with Guy, and the invention of New Jack Swing, his behind-the-scenes profile went overground and he became the most in-demand producer on the circuit. When Guy broke up in 1991, Riley worked with everyone from labelmates Heavy D and Mary J. Blige to Bobby Brown and Hammer, and was responsible for the only decent tracks on Michael Jackson's *Dangerous* album.

As Guy fans clamoured for a reunion, Riley formed a new group in 1994. Having recruited vocalists Chauncey "Black" Hannibal, Levi Little and Dave Hollister, Riley relocated from New York to Virginia Beach and started BLACKstreet as a return to classic soul. Although he called his new style "Heavy R&B", the first, self-titled, BLACKstreet album wasn't very different from the previous Guy material and tracks like "Before I Let You Go" and "Booti Call" were virtually indistinguishable from the deluge of swingbeat singles that followed in Guy's wake.

In 1995 Little and Hollister left to pursue solo careers and were replaced by Mark Middleton and Eric Williams. Anchored by one of *the* singles of the '90s, No Diggity, the second BLACKstreet album, **Another Level**, finally moved R&B away from the Guy and Babyface models. Although occasionally straying into the same overwrought territory that Aaron Hall (Guy's lead vocalist) bequeathed to R&B, *Another Level* was smooth without being too smarmy or too nasal, the beats had the funk but never slammed with hip-hop attitude; in fact, it sounded like a SWV album, but with guys singing.

As the samples on **Don't Leave Me** and **The Lord Is Real (Time Will Reveal)** indicate, Riley seems to have taken his lead from DeBarge. While not exactly as angelic or pristine as DeBarge, on *Another Level* Hannibal, Middleton and Williams inject some falsetto levity into the he-man parameters laid out by Hall. Meanwhile, Riley's production floats more than it bumps: absorbing both DeBarge and Stevie Wonder (check out the synth solo on "Don't Leave Me" that imitates Wonder's harmonica), he finally makes peace with the slow jam and mostly ditches the frenetic synthscapes of old. Tracks like **I Can't Get You (Out of My Mind)**, **Never Gonna Let You Go** and **I Wanna Be Your Man** could be early '70s quiet storm numbers right down to their narrative interludes, squishy Fender Rhodes licks and Grover Washington Jr. samples – the only things they're missing are some thunderclaps and rain sounds. Where Guy broke with soul by embracing hip-hop and urban noise, *Another Level* is a retreat to the make-out couch of Teddy Pendergrass and the Chi-Lites, far away from the stress and strife of the city.

On **Fix** Riley even manages to turn one of the hallmarks of hip-hop's engagement with ghetto chaos (the keyboard riff from Grandmaster Flash and the Furious Five's "The Message") into an instrumental chat-up line promising a night of essential oil rubdowns, scented candles and athletic sex. Elsewhere, on **This Is How We Roll**, Riley takes Montell Jordan's "This Is How We Do It", slows down the pace to a crawl, adds some Barry White keyboards and after-hours saxuality and metamorphoses an over-excited, hip-hop dry hump into a slow and steady eargasm.

The reason *Another Level* went quadruple platinum, though, was "No Diggity". With its brilliant Bill Withers sample, melismatic come-ons and head-nodding beats, "No Diggity" was everything the merger of hip-hop and soul promised. It might just be Riley's finest moment and, ironically, is actually what Guy would have sounded like if they reformed in the mid-'90s.

⟐We almost chose **BLACKstreet**, Interscope, 1994

Bobby "Blue" Bland

Two Steps from the Blues

Duke, 1962

Ray Charles generally gets most of the credit, but if there is a record that definitively marks the transition from R&B to soul, it's Bobby "Blue" Bland's **Two Steps from the Blues**. The title says it all: with its horn-fuelled arrangements, gospel shouting and classic pop phrasing, *Two Steps from the Blues* is a couple of rungs up the evolutionary ladder from the traditional delta blues, and represents the sharp right turn from the blues continuum that characterised Southern soul.

Bland's career began as a member of the fabled Beale Streeters, a group of Memphis bluesmen that included B.B. King, Johnny Ace and Rosco Gordon. Although Ike Turner and Sam Phillips had lent their typical intensity to his earliest solo records, Bland's heart was closer to the mellow blues styles of T-Bone Walker and Ace than to the brimstone and fire approach of the Sun Studio – with the exception of Sam Cooke, no other secular singer was as obviously influenced by gospel as he was. The irony is that Bland's success came from the tension between these two approaches – the smooth big-band blues sound and hard gospel testifying. Bland's vocal power, learned from listening to the Dixie Hummingbirds and Reverend C.L. Franklin, was gradually harnessed by arranger/trumpeter Joe Scott, who encouraged him to learn Nat "King" Cole-style phrasing. The ensuing combination of pop economy and gospel force, stately grace and down-on-his-knees pleading made Bland the harbinger of Otis Redding, Percy Sledge, James Carr, Wilson Pickett and Joe Tex.

Scott not only taught Bland pop vocal techniques; he also surrounded his cavernous voice with arrangements that dragged the blues kicking and screaming through Tin Pan Alley. Scott used strings, countrypolitan choirs, bizarre organs, massed brass and, later on, rumbas to create the blend of the blues, gospel, country and pop that would coalesce as soul. Of course, there are still out-and-out blues touches on *Two Steps*, but the blend that Scott and Bland achieved was clearly something else: a fusion that made Tony Bennett as gut-wrenching as Robert Johnson and Julius Cheeks as smoky and mellow as Charles Brown.

Cry Cry Cry epitomises the album's approach. Starting off as a fairly typical B.B. King urban blues shuffle, the song builds in intensity as Bland's melisma gets stronger. After Bland testifies his broken heart out, the arrangement shifts focus to a tinkling cocktail piano riff, only to speed up the tempo again to another exorcism of the demon of unrequited love. I'm Not Ashamed follows with the kind of 1950s rock'n'roll piano holdover and guitar comping that would characterise Arthur Alexander records, while Don't Cry No More is Bland's version of early James Brown. Lead Me On has Bland crooning on top of a flute obbligato, warbling Nelson Riddle strings and the kind of singers Ray Charles would use on *Modern Sounds in Country and Western Music*. This Perry Como move is followed by the seriously sinister I Pity the Fool, which predated Mr. T by some two decades.

Two Steps may be stylistically schizophrenic, but it all hangs together in a way that few albums of the period did. Its centrepiece Little Boy Blue (released as a single in 1958) sounds as if it took all the antipathy between blues musicians and gospel practitioners and packed it into two and a half minutes of the fiercest catharsis on vinyl. Bland's churchy squall is doubled the entire way by strafing axe licks from Pat Hare, creating one of the most intense records ever and making soul's supplanting of the blues inevitable.

⮑ We almost chose **I Pity the Fool: The Duke Recordings**, MCA, 1992

Mary J. Blige

My Life

Uptown/MCA, 1994

 Mary J. Blige is the undisputed "Queen of hip-hop soul" but, unlike the original Queen of Soul, Aretha Franklin, Blige's destiny as *the* female singer of her generation wasn't predetermined from childhood. Everyone knew Aretha would be a superstar the moment she started singing in her father's church choir in Detroit; Blige, on the other hand, was a high-school dropout from the housing projects of Yonkers, New York, with a rough demo tape that, somehow, found its way into the hands of Andre Harrell, the boss of Uptown Records.

Where Aretha was blessed with a gorgeous instrument, Blige often sings with a rasp that isn't coarse so much as corrosive and she sounds as if she's doing irreparable damage to her vocal cords every time she opens her mouth. Aretha's soaring voice matched the lofty aspirations of the Civil Rights era, Blige's modest vocal gifts mean that her evocations of pain sound unadorned, a perfect match for a climate that demands that its artists "keep it real". It's this "realness" that makes her a star. Unlike, say, Lauryn Hill, who is just so damned perfect that she seems like the air-brushed creation of some Madison Avenue advertising executive, Blige is true ghetto fabulous: a tough chick from the streets with a plausible figure and a penchant for garish leather and ornate fingernails.

After Harrell heard her demo recording, a version of Anita Baker's "Caught Up in the Rapture", the 21-year-old Blige was signed immediately and paired up with producer Sean "Puffy"

Combs to make her debut album. *What's the 411?* shot her into the spotlight and sold three million copies. With guest raps from Brand Nubian's Grand Puba and the first sighting of Combs' karaoke-machine production style, the album marked the transition away from New Jack Swing to the fuller integration of elements that was hip-hop soul. Although it had less of an obvious hip-hop element, **My Life**, her second album, released in 1994, perfected the formula developed on *What's the 411?* and followed it to triple-platinum status.

While there are no raps (aside from a 22-second interlude from Keith Murray) on *My Life*, the music is hip-hop, pure and simple. The album's lead track, Mary Jane, is a reworking of the Mary Jane Girls' classic '80s groover, "All Night Long"; You Bring Me Joy rides on top large chunks of Barry White's "It's Ecstasy When You Lay Down Next to Me"; there are classic hip-hop breaks like Roy Ayers' "Sunshine" and Isaac Hayes' "Ike's Mood"; the snares really snap even when played by Chucky Thompson rather than sampled. Like most of Combs' productions, the sampling isn't subtle or innovative and the covers of Rose Royce's I'm Goin' Down and Aretha Franklin's (You Make Me Feel Like) A Natural Woman might as well have been replaced with the original versions.

Originality wasn't the point, however: "realness" was, and on that score the song choices and the production could not have been better. This isn't "realness" in the sense of grim, hip-hop verité, but a portrait of the pain and vulnerability hiding beneath the street sass and hypersexuality that has, for better or worse, become the standard image of urban femininity. The album's feel is summed up by the title track, a plea for people to look beyond the street attitude and get rid of all that "negative energy". And in No One Else, produced by Mr. Dalvin from Jodeci, Al Green's Martin Luther King-referencing "Free at Last" is reworked into a testament of good sex that epitomises hip-hop soul's new approach.

⮑ We almost chose **What's the 411?**, Uptown, 1992

Booker T. & the MG's

The Best of Booker T. & the MG's

Atlantic, 1994

With only New Orleans' the Meters and Motown's the Funk Brothers as competition, Booker T. & the MG's were soul music's greatest instrumental group. As the house band of the Stax label, they not only backed such gifted singers as Otis Redding, Sam & Dave, Wilson Pickett, Carla Thomas and Eddie Floyd, but were largely responsible for crafting the label's signature sound. In fact, their grits 'n' gravy approach to grooving was perhaps the most crucial element in Stax's success. Unlike similar house bands, Booker T. & the MG's weren't tied to the studio, and as the musicians on the Stax Revues, the multiracial lineup of the MG's was visual and aural proof that integration could work in the Mid-South.

Like most of the best things in life, Booker T. & the MG's got their start by accident. Guitarist Steve Cropper was in charge of Stax's recording sessions and, during a session with rockabilly singer Billy Lee Riley, the band – Cropper, keyboardist Booker T. Jones, bassist Lewis Steinberg and drummer Al Jackson Jr. – was jamming around a slow blues riff entitled Green Onions. Introducing itself with perhaps the most memorable Hammond organ chords ever, "Green Onions" contained all the elements that would characterise the Stax sound: simple organ patterns, instantly memorable guitar punctuations, and a deceptively basic, but incredibly swinging, rhythm courtesy of one of the greatest drummers who ever lived. "Green Onions" eventually sold 700,000 copies and reached #3 on the US pop charts.

While the MG's would continue to have moderate success with instrumentals like the searing Tic-Tac-Toe and Soul Dressing (which could easily sit alongside the Amboy Dukes and the Litter in a compilation of American garage punk from the 1960s), the band quickly developed into Stax's studio mainstays, and they couldn't concentrate on replicating the commercial success of "Green Onions" until 1965's Boot-Leg. With added horns from Mar-Keys Wayne Jackson and Charles Axton and a dirtier, bouncier bottom end, "Boot-Leg" championed an altogether funkier sound and was the group's first R&B Top 10 hit since "Green Onions". Part of the new sound was due to new bassist Donald "Duck" Dunn, who introduced a higher level of rhythmic sophistication and swing compared to Steinberg's rather pedestrian walking bass-lines.

Despite the incomparably *nastay* Red Beans and Rice (featuring the wildest and rawest drums of Jackson's career), the surprisingly moody, almost funereal reading of the Gershwins' Summertime, and the magnificent sleaze of the should-have-been frat party anthem Be My Lady, the MG's would have to wait until 1967 for their next big hit. Hip Hug-Her featured a monstrous organ hook, similar in feel to the one on "Soul Finger" by the Bar-Kays, and a pimp-strutting groove that took the record into the pop Top 40.

When Al Bell joined Stax with dreams of turning it into a model of black capitalism to rival Motown, the label severed its distribution deal with Atlantic in 1968. What this means for present-day consumers is that there is no perfect MG's collection available on the market. **The Best of Booker T. & the MG's** ends with their rather pointless cover of the Rascals' Groovin' – you'll have to look elsewhere for the bass-heavy, proto-dub of "Hang 'Em High", the adrenaline-fuelled bass-line of "Time Is Tight: and the eight-minute funk epic "Melting Pot".

⮑We almost chose **Melting Pot**, Stax, 1971

James Brown

20 All Time Greatest Hits

Polydor, 1991

Just by picking up this book and looking at this page means that you really need *Star Time*, the four-disc anthology of James Brown's career, which is probably the greatest album ever released. But if fiscal rectitude is an issue, then **20 All Time Greatest Hits** will serve you admirably well until you scrape enough cash together to get the real deal.

James Brown was born in a shack on the outskirts of Barnwell, South Carolina on May 3, 1933. Dancing for pennies as a sideline to picking cotton in his adopted hometown of Augusta, Georgia, Brown was arrested for breaking into a car to steal a coat when he was 15 years old. Paroled in 1952, Brown soon joined lifelong sidekick Bobby Byrd's band. Changing their name to the Flames, the band took over Little Richard's local dates when he hit the big time. The Flames garnered a local following due to Brown's irrepressible energy and acrobatics, and recorded Please Please Please at a local radio station in 1955. Signed to Syd Nathan's King/Federal label, Brown and the Flames would re-record the song at the label's studio in February 1956, giving them an R&B Top 10 success and resulting in a record that would become *the* shibboleth of soul with its co-mingling of raggedy religious fervour and sexual ecstasy bordering on dementia.

Before rewriting every rule about the role of rhythm in Western music, James Brown laid waste to the standard notion of a ballad singer – a feat perhaps even more important than his mutations of rhythm. Like that other funky megalomaniac,

George Clinton, Brown always wanted to be a crooner – in his fantasies he was a camel-walking cross between Louis Jordan and Billy Eckstine. But, as desperately as James wanted to be as urbane and smooth as Charles Brown, he was more like a rasping Roy Brown. Ray Charles may have introduced the sound of gospel into R&B, but Brown brought the speaking-in-tongues *possession* exhibited by such shouters as the Five Blind Boys of Mississippi's Archie Brownlee and the Sensational Nightingales' Julius Cheeks into popular music. When Brown applied his scorched-earth vocals to standards like "Bewildered" and "Prisoner of Love" (not included here) and actually made the pop charts, smarmy love men like Johnny Mathis must have been running for cover. Indeed, by the end of 1963, when Brown's godchildren Otis Redding and Wilson Pickett were right around the corner, Mathis was banished from the charts for fifteen years.

With James Brown the tiniest gesture – an "unnh", a "Good God", an off-the-cuff vamp – meant everything. No one, not even Phil Spector or Trevor Horn, has packed as much stuff – timbres, forward motion, sparkle, intensity, unnh – into every single bar. Even when Brown started to economise in the '70s, he always retained a keen sense of what made pop music great in the first place: an immediacy and momentum that steam-rollered any obstacles in their path. With this simplicity, Brown is at once the most superficial musician in history and the most profound: there is nothing below the surface of any of his performances, yet his links to a tradition a millennium old are glaringly obvious. The tectonic shift in rhythm that he began with "Out of Sight" and Papa's Got a Brand New Bag and perfected with Cold Sweat and Get Up (I Feel Like Being a) Sex Machine has left its imprint on everything, even modern classical music, that has followed, making James Brown not just the Godfather of Soul, but the most important man in show business.

⊃We almost chose **Star Time**, Polydor, 1991

James Brown

Foundations of Funk: A Brand New Bag
1964–1969

Polydor, 1996

No major musical figure has been treated better after the end of their peak than Mr. Dynamite. With the renewed interest in funk prompted by both hip-hop and Britain's rare groove movement, Polygram placed Brown's catalogue in the hands of scholars and former associates like Cliff White, Harry Weinger and Alan Leeds, who have produced a series of revelatory reissues that are landmarks of curatorial diligence and corporate largesse. Aside from *Star Time*, **Foundations of Funk** is the best of these compilations. Covering the first half of Brown's golden age (1964–69), *Foundations of Funk* chronicles Brown and band dismantling music's bottom end just as the Beatles were rearranging its top end.

With one ear on the street picking up the latest slang, and one ear on Jesse Hill's 1960 proto-funk classic "Ooh Poo Pah Doo", in May 1964 Brown crafted Out of Sight, a sinuous and sinewy groove that was as taut and lithe as his own dancing. As far away from Sam Cooke and Motown as "Out of Sight" was, nothing could have prepared the world for Papa's Got a Brand New Bag. As insistent as any punk song, "Papa"'s rhythmic sophistication changed the world by shifting the accent of the downbeat. While racists like to ascribe a "primal" and "natural" sense of rhythm to Brown, the bone-rattling effect of "Papa" was largely due to the fact that the master tape was sped up, thus giving the record a claustrophobic feel that made the blaring horns, piercing guitar and ricocheting rhythm section that much more intense. At the same time as "Papa" is all about glare and flamboyance (the horns, Brown reducing the gospel vocal tradition to nothing but the falsetto shrieks and guttural roars, the "chank" of the guitar which is probably the genesis of reggae), it also posits the once anonymous bottom end as the be-all and end-all of music.

He followed "Papa's Got a Brand New Bag" with the equally marvellous I Got You (I Feel Good), Money Won't Change You and Let Yourself Go. With the call-and-response interplay between guitarists Jimmy Nolen and Alphonso "Country" Kellum and the horn section on 1967's "Let Yourself Go", the guitar began to supplant the horns as the main instrumental focus in Brown's music. Nolen and Kellum were brought even further up front on the two records that definitively began the shift away from soul towards funk, Cold Sweat and There Was a Time. With the exception of the incomparably *nastay* Dyke & the Blazers, "Cold Sweat" sounded like nothing else that was around at the time: the "give the drummer some" interlude where drummer Clyde Stubblefield and bassist Bernard Odum invent most of the next thirty years' worth of music, the catchiest horn hook ever, and Brown using his own voice like he used the rest of the band – as a percussion instrument.

That's just what's on the first disc. The second might be even more remarkable, if only for the fact that the twelve cuts were all recorded in a year and two months from August 1968 to October 1969. 1969's Give It Up or Turnit a Loose was nothing more than a vamp with one horn lick, a bridge and Brown grunting the title phrase a few times, while that same year's Ain't It Funky was the same, but twice as long. During this time Brown also invented the fifteenth dance craze of his career, the popcorn, but this was really the time when the funk really started to take shape and when "Say It Loud – I'm Black and I'm Proud" made Brown Soul Brother #1.

⮌We almost chose **Sex Machine**, Polydor, 1970

James Brown

Live at the Apollo

Polygram, 1963

Recorded on October 24, 1962, **Live at the Apollo** is almost certainly the greatest live album ever. The album was pure physicality transposed to vinyl: flash, coruscating motion, bravado, urgency. Despite the rapturous crowd noise, listening to it was like spying on someone dancing in front of a bedroom mirror convinced of his own magnificence: Brown's presence was so great that it often felt like there was no one else in the theatre. That said, the only problem with *Live at the Apollo* – or, indeed, any of his live albums – was that when you heard the crowd screaming, you knew that you were missing Brown doing the mashed potatoes or good-footing it across the stage or throwing his cape off to come back one last time.

The hysteria that Brown generated during his shows was like a sanctified prayer meeting and nowhere else in soul's recorded legacy was the influence of the church as powerful and obvious as on *Live at the Apollo*'s epic **Lost Someone**. "Lost Someone" also featured the most succinct summation of Mr. Dynamite's career and appeal he has offered: "Don't just say, 'Ow', say, 'OOOWWWW!!'" With the exception of a few Tantric mystics, no one has mastered the art of pacing and delayed gratification like Brown: check the Medley which follows "Lost Someone" for a master course on teasing, punctuation and throwing the trump card at just the right time.

While Brown's energy and the ecstatic screams of the audience made the album, *Live at the Apollo* might also have been Brown's finest vocal performance. His singing – all rising dynamics and shaking melisma – on I Don't Mind and "Lost Someone" showed why Brown was the Godfather of Soul long before he was the Minister of the New, New Super Heavy Funk. Even more masterful, though, might have been the moment in the Medley where he modulated from the gospelese of I Want You So Bad to the Billy Eckstine suavity of I Love You, Yes I Do with one quavering note.

Playing some 300 dates a year (often with three or four shows a night), the James Brown Band was not only the hardest-working band in show business, but also the tightest. Brown ran his band like a US Marine drill sergeant, fining band members if they missed a note or if their shoes weren't shiny enough. Of course, the band's success wasn't just due to discipline; Brown was blessed with unique talents. Shining brightest on *Live at the Apollo* was drummer Clayton Fillyau. By combining the fonk of New Orleans street rhythms propagated by drummers like Charlie "Hungry" Williams and Smokey Johnson with the marching band patterns of his Florida roots, Fillyau is perhaps more responsible than anyone else for the "James Brown beat".

As great as *Live at the Apollo* is, it almost never happened. Convinced that his fans would want a document of his electric live show, Brown approached Syd Nathan about recording some concerts at Harlem's Apollo Theatre. Nathan steadfastly refused, but Brown went ahead and paid for the recording himself. Shelved until May 1963, *Live at the Apollo* would eventually hit #2 on the American album charts (prevented from reaching the top spot, ironically enough, by its diametric opposite, Andy Williams' *Days of Wine and Roses*) and stay in the charts for 66 weeks. Not only was *Live at the Apollo* a commercial and artistic triumph, but as the result of Brown's own business acumen the album, along with Ray Charles's growing independence, was a high-profile symbol of the viability of African-American self-sufficiency.

⮌We almost chose **Live at the Apollo Volume 2**, Rhino, 1968

Roy Brown

Good Rocking Tonight: The Best of Roy Brown

Rhino, 1994

Combining that characteristic, rollicking New Orleans swing with shrieks and squeals, Roy Brown has been called "the first singer of soul" by Crescent City R&B scholar John Broven. While he was certainly of the same jump-blues school as Louis Jordan and Wynonie Harris, Brown was less restrained (both musically and vocally) than any of his contemporaries and his style is a direct link to both rock-'n'roll and soul.

Brown was born in New Orleans in 1925, but spent a lot of time in both Texas and Los Angeles, where he tried to establish himself as a boxer. After finishing a club residency in Galveston, Texas, he returned to New Orleans in 1947 and recorded his most famous song, Good Rocking Tonight, for the Deluxe label. Although Wynonie Harris's faster, less jazzy version stole Brown's thunder, Brown's record was nearly as popular and charted in both 1948 and 1949. While Brown still displayed the restraint that was characteristic of the period, there was something approaching gospel melisma in his phrasing. He introduced shrieking into the blues shouter's vocabulary and his vocals influenced everyone from Little Richard and Elvis Presley to B.B. King, Bobby "Blue" Bland and James Brown. The follow-up records to "Good Rocking Tonight", Rockin' at Midnight and Boogie at Midnight, upped the swing quotient, and with the hand-clapping rhythms and killer sax solos they are as assuredly rock'n'roll as anything that came after.

From 1949 to 1951, nearly every one of Brown's records was a big R&B hit. By this point Deluxe had been bought by King Records, and Brown recorded his hot and blue **Butcher Pete** at the label's Cincinnati headquarters in November 1949. Despite the relocation, "Butcher Pete" was as frenzied and as swinging as anything concocted in New Orleans. 1950's **Hard Luck Blues** was a more straightforward slow blues number but Brown was no less at home here. He may not have had the range of the singers who followed his lead, but Brown had a marked influence on the urban blues style of B.B. King and Bobby Bland, and as the most committed singer outside of the church or the Mississippi Delta his passion and technique were a major contribution to the birth of soul.

The hits continued with **Cadillac Baby** and **Love Don't Love Nobody**, but 1951's **Big Town**, with its mix of cosmopolitan and downhome phrasing and mellow glissandi, was Brown's last significant hit for several years. By the end of 1951 Brown had been usurped by the electrified blues of B.B. King and by Northern harmony groups, like the Clovers and the Dominoes, who made the gospel connection explicit. Brown's records not only sounded too similar to each other, but, more importantly, they sounded old. His 1954 single, "Ain't No Rocking No More", sadly summed up his career at this point.

After a few years of solid, but old-fashioned, records for King, Brown returned to New Orleans, where he recorded for the Imperial label under the auspices of the great producer/arranger Dave Bartholomew. **Let the Four Winds Blow** managed to dent the American pop charts in 1957 on the strength of Brown's vocals and a classic New Orleans shuffle. Although it didn't sell at all, Brown's "Saturday Night" was another classic New Orleans rock'n'roll record, but by this point Brown was too old to be successful in the young person's world of rock'n'roll. His version of Buddy Knox's "Party Doll" was embarrassing and Brown's career was effectively over.

⊃We almost chose **Blues Deluxe**, Charly, 1993

Cameo

The Best of Cameo

Polygram, 1993

Although they will probably only be remembered for their one truly transcendent moment, the 1986 single Word Up, Cameo were actually one of the most innovative groups of the '80s. Taking funk in hitherto unimagined directions, Cameo were one of the very few bands to acknowledge the influence of hip-hop and respond to it without pandering to lowest-common-denominator commercial instincts. While bands like Kraftwerk, Yellow Magic Orchestra, P-Funk and Afrika Bambaataa had already explored the possibilities of the synthesizer, Cameo – with their angular and splintered soundscapes – were almost certainly the first group to truly apprehend the synthesizer's effect on rhythm tracks of the future.

Cameo's main man Larry Blackmon began the '70s as a Juilliard School student who played drums on sessions for the cult proto-disco group, Black Ivory. He then joined the thirteen-piece funk troupe New York City Players, who were heavily influenced by the Parliafunkadelicment Thang. After a single called "Find My Way", the group was renamed Cameo and released the compellingly minimalistic Rigor Mortis towards the end of 1976. Cameo's early output didn't stray too far from the model of most funk bands, however: long, mostly instrumental vamps based around a serpentine bass-line and chicken-scratch guitar that masked the cloying, smarmy sweetness of their wretched ballads.

Cameo didn't hit their stride until the release of I Just Want to Be in 1979. With its clever use of synthesizers, near-robotic backing singers and cryptic sociopolitical commentary, "I Just Want to Be" became one of the blueprints for black music in the '80s and Cameo continued to push dance music towards a future of jagged edges and sharp contours. 1980's Shake Your Pants, with its squiggles, wiggles and farting bass-lines, refined the vision of P-Funk's keyboard player, Bernie Worrell, but it was Flirt that would truly establish much of '80s R&B in Cameo's image. Borrowing a guitar line from Prince, "Flirt" remade funk as a chopped-up groove with shards of synth effects flying around the mix; it was as if Jamaican dub pioneer King Tubby had remixed a P-Funk track using one of UTFO's drum machines.

Under this hip-hop influence, Cameo pilfered a synthesized Ennio Morricone riff from Jonzun Crew's 1983 single, "Space Cowboy", using it on 1984's She's Strange and on 1985's Single Life. "She's Strange" was the group's first R&B #1 and one of the most original singles of the decade (unfortunately the version on The Best of Cameo is the far-less-inspired rap mix). On both tracks, the famous whistle from the soundtrack to *The Good, The Bad and the Ugly* lends a sense of ghost-town menace to Cameo's ultramodern sound – an implicit indictment of Reagan's abandonment of the inner city to outlaw gangs of thieves and drug dealers. The politics were writ larger on Talkin' Out the Side of Your Neck, a vicious anti-establishment rant that once again borrowed Prince's post-Hendrix guitar.

With the group whittled down to a trio of Blackmon, Nathan Leftenant and Tomi Jenkins, Cameo created their lasting anthem in 1986. A Top 10 single across the world, "Word Up" featured Blackmon's exaggerated, nasal vocals (created by using a battery of filters) uttering oblique lyrics like "We don't have time for psychological romance". Like its nearly as good follow-up, Candy, "Word Up" was really a brittle synth-dub that created a snare sound that would define the latter half of the '80s. Unfortunately, as their name suggests, Cameo's peak period was all too brief and their innovations would be perfected elsewhere.

⊃We almost chose **Word Up!**, Atlanta Artist, 1986

James Carr

The Essential James Carr

Razor & Tie, 1995

The epitome of "deep soul", James Carr has a voice so cavernous you can't find the bottom. With his booming gospelese begging, cry-in-your-beer country-style lyrics and mostly white backing musicians, Carr's records are among the finest examples of "country soul". However, Carr remains an obscurity to all but the biggest soul fans, and his is one of the saddest stories in a genre littered with unhappy endings.

Carr was born in 1942 in Mississippi but moved to Memphis soon afterwards. He got his musical training in church and his vocal style from listening to Julius Cheeks belting out hosannas with the Sensational Nightingales. As a singer with the gospel group the Harmony Echoes, Carr met his future manager and lifelong ally Roosevelt Jamison in the early '60s. Jamison convinced Carr to go secular and introduced him to Quinton Claunch's Goldwax label.

Despite his gospel credentials, Carr's first record, 1964's **You Don't Want Me**, was an urban blues side in the style of B.B. King and Bobby "Blue" Bland – albeit with more gravel and more drive in his voice. A few more lacklustre records followed until 1966's **You've Got My Mind Messed Up**. With its tick-tocking drum track, hungover horns and Otis Redding mimicry, the record was a complete Stax derivative, but with Carr's presence gradually asserting itself. In the opening passage Carr is a dead ringer for Redding, but as the song builds he exerts an imposing authority, and the break-down shrieks as the song fades out have an intensity only matched by a hard gospel singer like Julius Cheeks or Solomon Womack of the Swan Silvertones.

If "You've Got My Mind Messed Up" became a Top 10 R&B hit because of its resemblance to Redding, Love Attack should have done even better. Although it stalled just outside the R&B Top 20, "Love Attack" had Carr copying Redding's mannerisms as well as his timbre. After his next single, however, Redding would be borrowing from him. With Pouring Water on a Drowning Man, Carr became his own man and the song remains one of the masterpieces of Southern soul. Conjuring up both baptism and the womb, the prevailing immersion metaphor isn't all pain as Carr's laugh towards the end seems to suggest. Although previously recorded by Percy Sledge, Carr imbues the song with a power that no one else has approached.

As great as "Pouring Water on a Drowning Man" was, Carr's masterpiece is his version of Chips Moman and Dan Penn's definitive cheating song, The Dark End of the Street. While most of Carr's records are dominated by the unremitting power of his voice, here he is restrained, resigned to the fact that his love affair can never be made public. Backed by an echoplexed cathedral of sound from the house band at Chips Moman's American Sound Studio, this is a near-perfect performance of one of the greatest songs ever written.

"The Dark End of the Street" only reached #77 on the pop chart, but it has since been covered by everyone from Clarence Carter to the Flying Burrito Brothers and its legacy is secure. Unfortunately, Carr's is not. Throughout his brief career he was beset by emotional problems, which were exacerbated by drugs. Carr would go into near-catatonic states in the studio and on stage and he vanished from sight after a 1971 single with Atlantic went nowhere. This collection was the first time that his Goldwax singles were made available in his home country since their original release, and should go some way towards building the reputation of one of soul's unknown greats.

⮑ We almost chose **The Complete James Carr Volume 1**, Goldwax, 1993

The Jimmy Castor Bunch

The Everything Man: The Best of the Jimmy Castor Bunch

Rhino, 1995

Despite a career that extends back to the days of doo-wop, Jimmy Castor is one of soul's most underappreciated figures. Perhaps his position on the sidelines of soul history is due to his penchant for novelty numbers that have been marginalised as the modern-day equivalent of hokum jive. Or perhaps it's that his It's Just Begun unwittingly sowed the seeds of classic soul's demise by laying the breakbeat foundation of hip-hop. Whatever, the truth is that **The Everything Man** has one of the finest examples of the mastodon bass-line and thoroughly deserves a place in the soul/R&B pantheon.

Castor was born in Harlem in 1943. As a nasal lead vocalist, he fronted Jimmy & the Juniors, who recorded a couple of sides for the Mercury subsidiary Wing in 1956, but the group's debut single, I Promise to Remember, stalled when the Castor-penned tune was covered by Frankie Lymon & the Teenagers and entered the Top 10. The following year, Castor took over from Lymon as lead vocalist for the Teenagers. After a stint with them, he worked as a session saxophonist in the New York area – most famously on Dave "Baby" Cortez's roller-rink organ classic from 1962, "Rinky Dink".

Castor's reign as the clown prince of Harlem would begin in earnest in the mid-'60s with the boogaloo craze. Combining Latin percussion with soul's driving bass-lines, boogaloo took over America's dance floors, particularly New York's, with its huge Hispanic community. Castor's contribution to the craze was an inspired piece of jive called **Hey, Leroy, Your Mama's Callin' You**. With a timbale groove to die for (played by Castor) and a mambo piano vamp, "Hey, Leroy" was more explicitly Latin in feel than most boogaloo records and reached #31 in the American Top 40. More Latin soul records, like **Southern Fried Frijoles** and "Leroy's in the Army", followed, but failed to chart.

Six years later, however, Castor would re-emerge with a record that would make Larry Graham's fuzztone bass with Sly & the Family Stone sound tame. **Troglodyte (Cave Man)** had a brontosaurus bass groove that fitted perfectly with its theme and title. Combining the most bottom-heavy bottom end ever with distorted guitar riffs, the most-sampled intro of all time ("What we're going to do here is go back, way back . . .") and a stoopid tale about Neanderthal sexuality, "Troglodyte" was Castor's biggest record, reaching #6 on the US charts. Even better and much more important was **It's Just Begun**, which was featured alongside "Troglodyte" on his *It's Just Begun* album from 1972. While "It's Just Begun" was a killer funk groove with lyrics about the energies of youth, what made the record was its "break", where all the instruments dropped out except for the timbales and wah-wah guitar. This section of the record was played to death by block-party DJs like Kool Herc and Afrika Bambaataa and became one of the cornerstones of hip-hop.

"It's Just Begun" was Castor's greatest moment and would ensure his immortality, but his popularity on the streets would continue with **Say Leroy (The Creature from the Black Lagoon is Your Father)** (a sublime piece of dozens testifying on top of a spacy Latin soul groove), "Bertha Butt Boogie" (a reprise of the character from "Troglodyte"), the proto-disco of "Potential", and the devastating clavinet riff of "King Kong". Castor's hits dried up in the late '70s just as the genre he unintentionally helped create started making its own noise. But, as the embodiment of postwar New York music (from doo-wop through soul, Latin soul, funk and disco to hip-hop), Castor will remain one of soul music's titans.

⮑We almost chose **Hey, Leroy, Your Mama's Callin' You**, Collectables, 1995

Ray Charles

The Best of Ray Charles: The Atlantic Years

Rhino, 1994

Billy Ward & the Dominoes, the Clovers and the "5" Royales all released records that revealed the influence of gospel well before Ray Charles. But it was Charles who got the credit for inventing soul and changing the course of music history, by incorporating gospel vocal techniques and instrumentation into the small-combo R&B style of the late 1940s and early '50s. It's not who gets there first that matters, however. Unquestionably, it was Charles's records that were the most startling and had the greatest effect. While Clyde McPhatter, Buddy Bailey and Johnny Tanner were all good singers, Charles was one of the half a dozen greatest singers in popular music. While his nimble swing and suggestive grunts and groans liberated libidos throughout the world, his country recordings of the '60s exposed a dirty little secret – that the nasal twangs and weepy timbres of country music were based on, and developed in close contact with, the black American music of the turn of the century. Whether you consider him merely an important formal stylist or an epochal figure in American cultural history, Ray Charles more than deserves his epithet, "The Genius".

After going blind at the age of 6, Charles was sent to the St. Augustine School for the Deaf and Blind, where he got his musical training. After several records that were largely derivative of Nat "King" Cole and Charles Brown, Charles signed with Atlantic Records, for whom he recorded some fun, jivey material before a 1954 session in Atlanta proved a turning point both in his career and in the history of popular music. Working with his own band, Charles arranged and produced the session himself: the result was **Come Back Baby/I've Got a Woman** – one of the two or three most significant singles ever released. With the galloping, Holy-Roller rhythm track and vocal swoops of "I've Got a Woman" and the pleading singing and churchy piano figures of "Come Back Baby" (lifted straight from the gospel standard "Move On Up a Little Higher"), the single couldn't have been more different from the stylised urbanity of his previous records, and marked the true beginnings of soul music.

Charles continued to push the gospel elements to the fore. His arrangement of **Drown in My Own Tears** could have come from any Southern Baptist church with Charles's stunning vocals leading the congregation of saxes and backing vocals towards the secular baptism of the song's title. **Hallelujah I Love Her So** begins with a piano part almost identical in style to the work of Mildred Falls, Mahalia Jackson's longtime accompanist. "Leave My Woman Alone" has a rhythm lifted wholesale from the gospel standard "Old Landmark", while the song's flip, **Lonely Avenue**, features the first appearance of vocal group the Cookies (later known as the Raeletts), who enhance the Sunday-morning atmosphere of Charles's recordings. The vocal interplay between Charles and lead Raelett, Margie Hendrix, is the defining characteristic of Charles's greatest record, 1959's **What'd I Say**, and the almost as good **Tell the Truth**.

After shocking and delighting the world in about equal measure with his heretical singing, and by the sexual frankness which was one of the hallmarks of the new genre, Charles set out to lay waste to both American standard melodies and country music. While many of these recordings have fine qualities by this point – the early '60s – soul was being more strongly advanced elsewhere and Charles would soon become the cabaret act that he remains to this day.

⮏We almost chose **The Birth of Soul**, Rhino, 1991

Chic

C'est Chic

Atlantic, 1978

chic cheer   i want your love
le freak   at last i am free
savoir faire   sometimes you win
happy man   (funny) bone

The second best band of the 1970s (after Parliament/Funkadelic) originally called themselves the Big Apple Band and played a ferociously metallic brand of Miles Davis-esque jazz fusion. In 1976, with the disco boom in full swing, guitarist Nile Rodgers, bassist Bernard Edwards and drummer Tony Thompson recruited vocalists Alfa Anderson and Norma Jean Wright to produce a sardonic dance-floor anthem called "Dance, Dance, Dance". With tongues firmly in cheek, they called themselves Chic and proceeded to shop the demo. After a string of rejections, the record was finally picked up by Atlantic. Over a galloping rhythm, Anderson and Wright intoned the title phrase like deer caught in the headlights. To drive the point home, they borrowed Gig Young's catch phrase ("Yowsah, yowsah, yowsah") from the film *They Shoot Horses, Don't They?*, Sidney Lumet's attack on the American psyche that uses a dance marathon as its setting. Typically of the mind-set which these art-rockers-at-heart were lampooning, no one got the joke and "Dance, Dance, Dance" reached #6 on the American charts in 1977.

While their record was riding high in the charts, Rodgers and Edwards decided to celebrate at Studio 54. When they couldn't get in – even though their record was being played inside – the two went back to the studio to work out some aggression. They came up with a snarling, popping funk vamp that even James Brown wouldn't have touched and, with Studio 54's bouncers in mind, called it "Fuck Off". A few days later, after they had calmed down, the chant "Aaahhh, fuck off!" became "Aaahhh, freak out!", and one of the best-selling singles of all time was born. The words might have changed, but the attitude was still there. Disembodied vocals mock the disco-as-liberation ethic with odd, stilted language sung in a deadpan style: "Night and days, uhhh, stomping at the Savoy/Now we freak, oh what a joy", "Big fun to be had by everyone/It's up to you, surely it can be done". Yet again, Chic had it both ways – treating their audience with as much scorn as the Sex Pistols, but still managing to sell some six million copies of Le Freak.

"Le Freak" anchored **C'est Chic**, but, as if to prove once and for all that they weren't a real disco group, the conceptual genius and impossible grooves continued through the entire record. Like the Roxy Music fans they were, Rodgers and Edwards dressed the band up in Halston, Gucci, Fiorucci and laid the ambiguity/distance shtick on thick. At Last I Am Free continued where "Le Freak" left off, only with a crawling tempo and Anderson and Martin (sounding alternately like zombies and angels), chanting the mantra, "At last I am free/I can hardly see in front of me". Even more of a sincantation and just as caustic was Chic Cheer, a five-minute vamp with fake crowd noise, heavily miked cymbals and the cheerleaders at Disco High exhorting the crowd, "If you're fans of Chic/Consider yourself unique". Chic's great theme would be the disco lifestyle's inherent fatalism and I Want Your Love was one of their finest love-as-addiction tales, complete with gloomy bells and an itching guitar part that never gets relieved.

For all their smarts and oddball touches, though, it was the grooves that everyone listened to. Rodgers was a great rhythm-guitar player and Bernard Edwards was certainly one of the five most creative bass players ever. With Tony Thompson, "the human metronome", behind them, the two distilled and updated Motown, James Brown, Stax and Miles Davis into the most lethal rhythmic attack of the last quarter century.

⤷We almost chose **Dance, Dance, Dance – The Best of Chic**, Atlantic, 1991

Chic

Risqué

Atlantic, 1979

Rock fans used to talk about disco denizens as if they were lemmings marching to the cliffs, while soul patrons lampooned them as robots who were faking the funk. Chic were criticised for producing escapist music even though pop music is meant to be all about escape in the first place. Anyway, the mid- to late 1970s demanded that kind of music, particularly in New York. In a climate of stagflation, when the country at large was being held hostage by the oil barons, when NYC owed fealty to the bond-issuing robber barons who bailed the city out of bankruptcy, when the mercenary laissez-faire capitalism of the '80s was just starting to take hold, when Reagan and the rollback of Civil Rights legislation was just around the corner and without the moral consensus of the '60s, the only possible reaction was escapism. But Chic were never just about escape. While they enjoyed shaking their groove thing as much as anybody, they also recognised hedonism's limitations and saw its dangers.

The group's third album, **Risqué**, led off with disco's crowning achievement, Good Times. A brilliant single which worked perfectly in the context of the album, it was also one of the most influential records of the time, helping to kick off hip-hop through its use on Sugar Hill Gang's "Rapper's Delight" and Grandmaster Flash's "The Adventures of Grandmaster Flash on the Wheels of Steel", and was ripped off almost note for note by Queen's "Another One Bites the Dust". Like all of their best work, Chic had it both ways on "Good Times". With Bernard Edwards' stunning bass-line, distilling the history of the electric bass into one groove, and Nile Rodgers' seething guitar work, the record bumped like a mother. However, the scything strings and ghostly piano gave the game away. With vocalists Alfa Anderson and Luci Martin intoning catch phrases like they were in a valium haze, the pep rally that "Good Times" were here seemed harder and harder to believe. Its evocation of the good life ("Clams on the half shell and rollerskates, rollerskates") was so absurd that not even Carly Simon would have sung the lyrics seriously. Then, when they repeat the second chorus, the song's sense of impending doom and the dread hidden beneath the surface becomes clear: "A rumor has it that it's getting late/Time marches on, just can't wait/The clock keeps turning, why hesitate?/You silly fool, you can't change your fate".

During the disc's second half, sadism keeps cropping up in the lyrics ("Love is pain and pain could be pleasure", "The way you treated me, you'd think I were into S&M", "Used me, abused me/Knocked down and walked all over me"). Even more revealing are the lines, sounding like slogans at a political rally or extracts from the transcripts of the Iran–Contra trial, that leap out fully formed from the disembodied vocals: "Now you've got yours, what about me?", "That sinister appearance and the lies/Whew, those alibis".

The filler fluff of **A Warm Summer Night** is the only breath of fresh air on the album: the rest deals with the impossibility of changing your fate and rails against sadistic lovers – a more perfect metaphor for the Thatcher–Reagan era would be hard to find. Accompanied by strings that sound like the shower sequence stabs from Bernard Hermann's score for *Psycho*, Anderson and Martin sing the title phrase of "My Feet Keep Dancing" over and over again like a mantra. It's as if they were either hypnotised or thought that by repeating the phrase so many times they'd keep the bogeyman away. Maybe they were right about the lemmings.

⮌We almost chose **Real People**, Atlantic, 1980

George Clinton

Computer Games

Capitol, 1982

After the platinum success of Funkadelic's *One Nation Under a Groove* album, George Clinton's P-Funk empire rapidly crumbled. With his fantasy of freak multitudes under his sway on both *One Nation* and the follow-up, *Uncle Jam Wants You*, Clinton seemed obsessed with himself as a superstar. His delusions of grandeur coincided with the band's hectic workload and protracted legal wrangles. Key musicians left to make albums as Quazar and Mutiny, while longtime associate Fuzzy Haskins tried to wrest control of the Funkadelic name; Parliament's label, Casablanca Records, was in financial turmoil; and Warner Bros. refused to sanction the phallo-rocket cover art for *Electric Spanking of War Babies*, allegedly only pressing 80,000 copies even though the previous two Funkadelic albums sold over a million copies each.

After the lacklustre single-entendres of Parliament's *Gloryhallastoopid* and *Trombipulation* and with the P-Funk nomenclature in legal turmoil, Clinton managed to release a "solo" project in 1982. With help from funkateers Bootsy Collins, Garry Shider, Junie Morrison and Bernie Worrell, the swansong of the Parliafunkadelicment Thang as a unified entity became perhaps the phenomenon's most enduring record. Although it inexplicably never made the pop chart, the second single from **Computer Games**, Atomic Dog, was an American R&B #1 for a month, while its rhythm loop – a classic P-Funk handclap appended to a backwards drum machine – and its "Why must I feel like that?/Why must I chase the cat?/Nothin' but the dog in me" refrain have remained in the language of R&B ever since. "Atomic Dog" was the perfect rapprochement of R&B's past with its future: harmony group chops coexisted with proto-rap vocals, while tried-and-tested grooves shared space with technological sophistication.

Even more conscious of its position as a transition record was the album's first single, Loopzilla. With a shout-out to Afrika Bambaataa ("Like planet rock/we just don't stop"), Motown quotations, video-game samples, synth licks, timbale breaks and mechanical rhythm loops, "Loopzilla" directly linked P-Funk with the new breed of funkateers like Prince and the Minneapolis mob, Gap Band, Yarbrough & Peoples, John Robie and a whole generation of hip-hop and electro artists whose blend of machinery and rump-shake was made possible by Parliament's "Flash Light".

In addition to gracefully passing the torch to a new generation, *Computer Games* also contained plenty of the classic P-Funk elements. Get Dressed was a serious funk spank that combined jive talkin', JB horns, Bernie Worrell's space-age keyboards and the kind of effects-pedal-mixing-board-drum-machine-synthesizer mumbo jumbo that still sounds futuristic even though it was made with equipment obsolete ten years ago. Pot Sharing Tots was probably Clinton's most deranged, most gratuitous love song throwaway, while *Computer Games* updated the prototype Funkadelic guitar sound by throwing in bits of Walter/Wendy Carlos Moog effects.

Although he had intermittent, mostly critical, success after *Computer Games*, Clinton's momentum was lost to the bands that brought the P-Funk blueprint into the '80s. Despite making great groove records like the 1983 *Urban Dancefloor Guerrillas* album by the P-Funk All Stars and his follow-up to *Computer Games, You Shouldn't-Nuf Bit Fish*, Clinton's name was dirt in the music industry and legal catastrophes seemed to follow him around wherever he went. Nonetheless, *Computer Games* stands as testament to the debt that everyone who followed owes to Clinton and his P-Funk Thang.

⤴We almost chose **P-Funk All Stars – Urban Dancefloor Guerrillas**, CBS, 1983

The Clovers

The Very Best of the Clovers

Rhino/Atlantic, 1998

As the western half of postwar America was jumping to the hepcat blues of Louis Jordan, Wynonie Harris and Ella Mae Morse, folks east of the Mississippi were grooving to the smoother sounds of the vocal groups inspired by the Ink Spots and the Charioteers. The Orioles were the best of these new vocal groups and their gorgeous 1948 single, "It's Too Soon to Know", is one of the perennial choices as "the first rock'n'roll record". While the Orioles moved away from the classic pop stylisation of their mentors, lead vocalist Sonny Til still sang in the "cool" style even if it was more emotional than anything that had come before.

Largely inspired by the Orioles, the Clovers were one of the first vocal groups to really expand the genre's boundaries by incorporating influences from the blues and Southern gospel as well as classic pop. Formed as a trio in 1947 in Washington DC by Harold Lucas, Billy Shelton and Thomas Woods, the Clovers started out performing the usual ballads in a style derived from the Orioles and the Ravens. When their manager Lou Krefetz brought them to the fledgling Atlantic Records in 1950, the production team of Ahmet Ertegun and Jesse Stone persuaded them to sully their traditionally borne vocal group sound with blue-note slurs, Southern grit and gospel melisma. Along with the Midnighters discovering the spirit in the flesh of a girl named Annie, the Clovers' defiled choirboy purity opened the floodgates of rock'n'roll and prepared the ground for soul.

With a revised line-up of John "Buddy" Bailey, Harold Lucas, Harold Winley, Matthew McQuater and guitarist Bill Harris, the Clovers' first recording for Atlantic, **Don't You Know I Love You**, was recorded in February 1951. Sung by Bailey with a voice that was more urgent, gutsy and bluesier than Sonny Til, "Don't You Know I Love You" was a whole new exciting blend – a gently rolling Southern blues number with dirty sax runs in the background. This melding of Northern sophistication with Southern earthiness had never happened before, and the song remained in the #1 spot on the R&B charts throughout the spring of 1951.

Over the next two years the Clovers would dominate the R&B charts with **Fool, Fool, Fool** (#1), **One Mint Julep** (#2), **Ting-A-Ling** (#1), **I Played the Fool** (#3) and **Hey, Miss Fannie** (#2). Of these, "I Played the Fool" was a particularly significant recording, not only because it was the group's first successful ballad, but also because it set the stage for the doo-wop groups that would soon follow. In 1953, Bailey was called up for military service, but despite losing their distinctive voice the Clovers continued to have R&B success.

With the less urbane lead singer Charlie White, who had previously sung with the Dominoes, the group's **Good Lovin'**, **Lovey Dovey** (featuring the immortal line, "I really love your peaches, I'm gonna to shake your tree") and **Little Mama** all reached the Top 5. White was then replaced by Billy Mitchell, who sang lead on the great **Your Cash Ain't Nothin' but Trash** (#6). Bailey returned to the fold in 1955, but by this time the Drifters and Elvis had made R&B safe for white teenagers, and their definitive version of **Blue Velvet** only made #14 on the R&B chart. Although they released some great singles like the Elmore James-inspired **Down in the Alley**, they went nowhere and the group parted company with Atlantic. The Clovers' swan song, **Love Potion No. 9** for United Artists, was ironically their biggest pop chart hit, peaking at #23 in 1959.

➲We almost chose **Down in the Alley**, Rhino, 1991

Nat King Cole

The Nat King Cole Story

Capitol, 1960

Along with Louis Armstrong, James Brown, Chuck Berry and Miles Davis, Nat King Cole was the most important African-American musician of the 1940s and '50s. His achievements are extraordinary: a highly accomplished pianist of the late swing era, his trio was the first successful small jazz group and inspired the legendary trios of Art Tatum and Oscar Peterson. He was one of the most successful pop singers of the immediate postwar period and was the first black performer to be accorded his own TV programme.

He began his career by playing in his brothers' Chicago-based jazz band, Eddie Cole's Solid Swingers, before moving to Los Angeles, where he played in a revue band and then formed a trio with guitarist Oscar Moore and bassist Wesley Prince. The trio originally concentrated on Earl "Fatha" Hines-style swing instrumentals and some hipster jive, novelty vocal numbers, but a recording of Sweet Lorraine, made during the group's first sessions in 1940 and featuring Cole's creamy vocals, swiftly propelled him into the role of America's most popular crooner after Frank Sinatra, Bing Crosby and Perry Como.

Cole was not only the first true crossover star of American popular music, he also largely invented the notion of "cool". Years before Miles Davis gave birth to cool jazz, Cole repressed his feelings and his church roots behind a veneer of classical pop artifice, hip lingo and sharp suits. Like other great crooners, his smoothness suggested intimacy, but it was the sense that he was holding something back that gave his performances another dimension and, paradoxically, made his records more emotional. Everyone from Charles Brown to Ray Charles was influenced by Cole's style and, despite the eventual dominance of gospel's more visceral approach in the '60s, Cole's coolness still has its adherents, albeit in very different clothes. **The Nat King Cole Story** is a double-CD set which sees Cole revisiting the tracks that made him one of the greatest classic pop singers, often in superior versions to the originals.

Cole's first major hit was his first side for Capitol, Straighten Up and Fly Right in 1943, but it was his remake of "Sweet Lorraine" that same year that made his name. "Straighten Up and Fly Right" was a jivey, little Louis Jordan-style cut that had plenty of swing, while "Sweet Lorraine" was a restrained, bluesy ballad that showcased Cole's mixture of classic pop and blue notes. Other hits like It's Only a Paper Moon, (Get Your Kicks on) Route 66 and (I Love You) For Sentimental Reasons followed with similar combinations of finger-snapping propulsion and emotional reticence.

The turning point in Cole's career, however, was his version of Mel Tormé's The Christmas Song. Marrying pop's stylisation and good-life fantasies with faint echoes of jazz rhythms and blue notes, Cole's first record with orchestration, like Louis Armstrong's "What a Wonderful World", transcended its origins by sheer force of personality. Records like Nature Boy and his stunning version of Lush Life followed with masses of strings and Cole was becoming a pop star. Perhaps his most saccharine recording, Mona Lisa, put him over the top and Cole became one of America's biggest pop singers.

With the exception of sides like the Billy May collaboration, "Walkin' My Baby Back Home", and some inspired jazz recordings, Cole mostly abandoned any hint of R&B throughout the '50s in favour of mainstream pop arrangements. Although his short-lived television series in 1956–57 was of tremendous symbolic importance, Cole's best work was behind him and his innovations and role had been taken over by Johnny Mathis.

⟲We almost chose **Nat King Cole**, Capitol, 1992

Sam Cooke

Wonderful World

RCA, 1986

That Sam Cooke is one of the greatest singers in the history of recorded music is undeniable. Unfortunately, Cooke's glorious voice was all too often buried under some of the least sympathetic production imaginable. The standard explanation for this is that Cooke was the puppet of white pop Svengalis, but the truth is that – while he didn't arrange them – Cooke wrote most of his own songs himself. But if Cooke's determination to court as wide an audience as possible only produced a handful of good pop records, his efforts must be placed in the context of the 1957 American pop market, where Pat Boone still outsold Little Richard.

Cooke was born in Chicago in 1931, the son of a minister. He spent his entire youth singing in church and joined the Highway Q.C.'s, a group affiliated with the legendary Soul Stirrers. In 1950 he was picked by the Soul Stirrers to replace their enormously influential lead singer R.H. Harris and, like his predecessor, Cooke set out to change the rules of gospel. He was helped by his pin-up looks and sweet voice, which attracted legions of swooning teenage girls. Gospel had never seen anything like it, and with the very earthly metaphors of Cooke's composition, "That's Heaven to Me", his conversion to the devil's music became increasingly inevitable. In 1956, at a secret session Cooke recorded secular material, which was released under a pseudonym. The records didn't do anything – except succeed in estranging Cooke from his record label, the rest of the Soul Stirrers and the bulk of the gospel community. He left the fold in 1957.

When Cooke went secular, he went all the way: sickly strings, cumbersome arrangements too clunky even for a Vegas singer and chorales straight from the Mormon Tabernacle Choir songbook. Released in October 1957, **You Send Me** was Cooke's breakthrough. Ray Charles had already rocked the world with "I've Got a Woman", but no one was quite prepared for Cooke's floating "whoooaaahhh". No one outside of the gospel community had ever heard anything approaching the sensuousness of his singing and his description of ecstasy was miles away from the puppy love of the doo-wop singers. "You Send Me" topped both the pop and R&B charts and set in motion a string of 29 Top 40 hits over the next eight years.

Aside from Cooke's voice, though, these were hits that hearkened back to the old pre-rock'n'roll days. When Cooke left the Keen label for RCA in 1960, the Italian-American duo Hugo and Luigi took over production duties. Their overwrought and unswinging arrangements were perfectly suited to trifles like "Frankie and Johnny" and "Tennessee Waltz" (neither, thankfully, included here), but Cooke was always capable of transcending his material, and even as lame a song as **Chain Gang** is saved through the pure beauty of the voice. Among all the dreck, though, there were some sublime pop moments: **Wonderful World**, **Having A Party**, **Twistin' the Night Away**, "Soothe Me" and **Bring It on Home to Me**, the last couple of which would profoundly influence the direction of soul after his death.

Cooke's greatest record as a pop singer, however, was a two-sided single that was only released after his mysterious death outside a prostitute's hotel room. The A-side, "Shake", was a dance novelty featuring a rhumba rhythm and instructions to "Move your body like a whip". The flip was "A Change Is Gonna Come", a monumental record which, along with "Bring It on Home to Me", was the only time Cooke truly matched the profundity of his gospel records.

⮌ We almost chose **Live at the Harlem Square Club**, RCA, 1985

D'Angelo

Brown Sugar

EMI, 1995

Aside from Prince, the best soul of the 1980s and '90s was soul which dared to engage with hip-hop. The reason why **Brown Sugar** was the best soul album since *Sign o' the Times*, however, was that its hip-hop-invigorated R&B was anchored by the most traditional of soul virtues – a solid grounding in the church.

Born Michael D'Angelo Arthur in Richmond, Virginia, in 1975, D'Angelo is the son and grandson of preachers. Like the very best soul singers, D'Angelo transfers gospel's religious ecstasies to their real-world equivalent – the pleasures of the flesh. While old gospel albums were his inspiration on the making of *Brown Sugar*, he is also keenly aware of soul's own traditions. Although lumped in with the group of retro-soulsters like Maxwell, Lauryn Hill, Erykah Badu, Rafael Saadiq (who co-produced *Brown Sugar*'s Lady) and Tony Rich, D'Angelo is more than just a Marvin Gaye fetishist. Reproaching the new school of R&B for its overwhelming narcissism, D'Angelo – along with Hill – stands as a champion for soul's ability to communicate more complex ideas than knocking boots with a groupie in the back seat of a Lexus.

None of which is to say that D'Angelo's music isn't sexy; just that it doesn't mawl you like some overexcited 14-year-old whose idea of foreplay is thrusting his groin in your face. Perhaps indicative of this, *Brown Sugar* 's sexiest, and best, song is a smouldering ballad dedicated not to a lover, but to smoking the kind bud. Co-produced by A Tribe Called Quest's Ali Shaheed

Muhammad, **Brown Sugar** blends late-night Jimmy Smith-style organ, atmospheric percussion and snapping snares to create *the* soul song of the decade. Where Jodeci and their ilk were counting the notches on their bedposts, on "Brown Sugar" D'Angelo extols the pleasures of pot-fuelled solipsism ("Always down for a ménage à trois/But I think I'ma hit it solo/Hope my niggaz don't mind") and intimates that love, or at least love of the herb, leads to insanity ("Brown Sugar babe/I gets high off your love/I don't know how to behave"). **Jonz in My Bonz** compares love to addiction, with D'Angelo burying his moans and falsetto flights in an array of studio trickery.

The metaphors aren't all weed-inspired, however. **Me and Those Dreamin' Eyes of Mine** is about a man stuck in a fantasy and features D'Angelo singing in a quartet with all the voices in his head to reinforce the vibe. The tick-tocking drum-frame beat of the track leads right into the nastiest cheating song since that hoary old standard of '60s rock, "Hey Joe". **Sh*t, Damn, Motherf*cker** finds the singer walking in on his best friend and his wife in bed together, but instead of a narrative the song is just a string of exclamations and rhetorical questions, ending with D'Angelo wondering, "Why the both of you's bleeding so much?/Why am I wearin' handcuffs?" The punchy drums and biting wah-wah guitar riff drive the point home as the singer replays the scenario over and over again in his mind.

D'Angelo is just as good on the straight-up love songs. His cover of Smokey Robinson's **Cruisin'** is as good as, if not better than, the original and asks an important question in this age of downsizing: when was the last time you heard a real string section on an album? "Lady" brings a touch of paranoia to a plea to go public with their love, using the jazzy hallmarks of bohemian soul to emphasise the singer's insecurity. But however great the production is (all of it produced or co-produced by D'Angelo), what you really notice is that he's the finest singer since Prince.

⊃ We almost chose **Voodoo**, Virgin, 2000

Lee Dorsey

The Definitive Collection

Arista, 1997

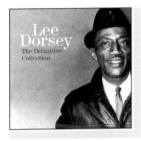

Called "the hidden jewel of soul" by Joe Strummer, Lee Dorsey has toured with the Clash, recorded with Southside Johnny and been name-checked by the Beastie Boys ("Everything I do is funky like Lee Dorsey" from "Sure Shot"). The reason for Dorsey's minor celebrity is simple: he's just about the hippest cat to ever shake his sacroiliac on vinyl. With his lazy drawl, comic timing, sly Ray Charles rips and Cajun *je ne sais quoi*, Dorsey is *the* voice of post-Fats Domino New Orleans. Combined with arrangements from Allen Toussaint and grooves from the best of the Crescent City's seemingly limitless talent pool, Dorsey's records are some of the crucial building blocks of "the fonk".

Born on Christmas Eve 1924, Dorsey was an old man in pop music terms when he first burst on the scene in 1961. In between he was a boxer calling himself Kid Chocolate (but he wasn't the famous Kid Chocolate) and working in a junkyard. He had recorded a couple of small singles like "Lottie Mo" (under the auspices of local legend Joe Banashak) that didn't get off the bayou, but they were heard by New York R&B men Marshall Sehorn and Bobby Robinson, who sensed that he was a special talent. Based on a schoolyard chant, Dorsey's first and biggest hit, Ya Ya, was written in half an hour in a bar in New Orleans by Robinson and Dorsey. Arranged by Allen Toussaint and Harold Battiste, "Ya Ya" rode Toussaint's infectious piano line and subtle second-line swing all the way to #7 on the American pop chart in 1961. Moving from sublime melisma to a ridiculous whoop in the span of a few notes, Dorsey's unaccompanied intro encapsulates his basic vocal approach.

Dorsey followed up "Ya Ya" on Robinson's Fury label with the almost-as-good **Do Re Mi** (which reached #27 in the Top 40), but by 1963 Robinson and his labels were in financial trouble and Dorsey disappeared back to New Orleans' Ninth Ward. Two years later he re-emerged on Toussaint and Sehorn's new Amy label with a single, **Ride Your Pony**, which was another Top 40 hit, and which helped re-establish the importance not only of the singer and producers, but of New Orleans as a whole. By then New Orleans had lost its status as America's capital city for R&B to Detroit and Memphis, but "Ride Your Pony" – stealing a riff and a groove from Motown's Junior Walker – helped reclaim the funk for its rightful home.

The following year Dorsey released the even more crucial **Get out of My Life Woman**. With the hottest of drumbeats (played by jazz skinman June Gardner) and a vocal oozing with Southern attitude, "Get out of My Life Woman" only made the lower reaches of the Top 100 but went on to inspire countless cover versions and to become one of the most sampled records in history. Dorsey's next single, **Working in the Coalmine**, featured another outrageously funky beat, but it was the great vocal arrangement and Dorsey's almost camp asides that made the record into an instant pop smash.

The hits dried up after 1966's **Holy Cow** but, with Toussaint and the Meters, Dorsey continued to release great records. 1969's **Everything I Do Gohn Be Funky** more than lived up to its title, with Dorsey and organist Art Neville getting mighty loose. Two tracks from his underrated album *Yes We Can*, "Sneakin' Sally Through the Alley" and "Yes We Can", find Dorsey somewhere below his vocal peak, but he's more than compensated for by some of the *nastayest* instrumental tracks ever recorded. Dorsey continued to release albums through the '70s, but sadly he succumbed to emphysema in 1986.

⊃We almost chose **Holy Cow! The Best of Lee Dorsey**, Arista, 1985

Dr. Buzzard's Original Savannah Band

Dr. Buzzard's Original Savannah Band

RCA, 1976

The first words that you hear on this album are "Zoot suit city"; the first couplet rhymes "if that would get me ovah" with "equivalency diploma"; the first sounds are the rum-tum-tum of the tom-tom and some Glenn Miller (not even Count Basie) brass razzle-dazzle. Clearly, this isn't your average get-the-dancers-on-the-floor-with-a-simple-4/4-beat, functional disco record.

For all the Cotton Club touches and Busby Berkeley glitz, **Dr. Buzzard's Original Savannah Band** isn't some tacky 1940s revival schmaltz like Taco's "Puttin' on the Ritz". Instead, fraternal co-conspirators August Darnell (aka Tommy Browder) and Stony Browder Jr. construct a fantasy world in which show tunes swing, the ghetto is filled with golden age Hollywood glamour, and heartbreak can be exorcised with a witty turn of phrase. Granted, on paper it sounds like the most retrograde, revisionist kind of record, but on the turntable it's one of the most fully realised, dazzling artefacts from the black bohemian intelligentsia and the first great single-artist disco.

Like everything produced by the brothers Browder (August Darnell would soon metamorphose into Kid Creole), *Dr. Buzzard's Original Savannah Band* teeters perilously on the edge of super-archness. However, Darnell's words are never so stilted or so camp that they fail to bring a smile to your face and Stony Browder's penguin-suited pastiche of the big-band era never quite disintegrates into rhinestone kitsch. For all the cleverness of the ring leaders, though, it's vocalist Cory Daye who steals the show. With her combination of Great White Way razzmatazz and uptown soul, Daye has perhaps the most likable, engaging vinyl persona of any female singer since the classic blues divas Bessie Smith and Alberta Hunter. Whether she's rolling her tongue à la Billy Stewart and Jackie Wilson, giving the lyrics some Rita Moreno sass or oo-poo-pah-dooing like Betty Boop, Daye almost single-handedly brings this record out of the art ghetto and into a warm and moving pop realm, albeit an impeccably stylish and hip one.

Daye does have some great material to work with, though. Taking his cue from Cole Porter, Darnell crafts some of the most bizarre, strikingly original and deliciously camp love and break-up songs ever written. He may fetishise the glory days of Tin Pan Alley, but there's nothing approaching "moon-June-spoon" here. Instead, we get lines like "I'll grow a tail or two for you/Spend the rest of my days locked up in a zoo", "They're all the same, the sluts and the saints" and "Now the sun must rise/With her bag of tricks and cheats and dirty lies". Of course, Browder's music helps: on tracks like Sour & Sweet/Lemon in the Honey and Cherchez La Femme the stylistic synthesis is so perfect that stomping at the Savoy and bumping at Studio 54 seem virtually identical activities. After you get used to the Cab Calloway shtick, you begin to notice the Latin rhythms and fantastic bass-line, and discover that beneath the children's chorus on Sunshower is a skeletal Nigerian juju track complete with Hawaiian guitar and talking drums.

A measure of this album's boldness and singularity is that the group even pokes fun at their label boss's love woes on "Cherchez La Femme": "Tommy Motola lives on the road/He lost his lady two months ago . . . He sleeps in the back of his big gray Cadillac, blowing his mind on cheap grass and wine". But for all of the industry name-dropping, internal rhymes and posing on *Dr. Buzzard's Original Savannah Band*, what matters most is that these fashion-mag wannabes have created a record that is as moving and as smart as any other album in the history of soul.

⮌ We almost chose **Dr. Buzzard's Original Savannah Band Meets King Pennet**, RCA, 1978

The Drifters

Rockin' and Driftin': The Drifters Box

Rhino, 1993

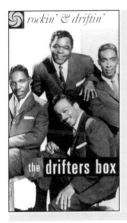

The Drifters are quite simply the greatest of all R&B vocal groups, responsible, more than anyone else, for the transition of R&B to soul. While the Drifters counted two of the greatest R&B stylists – Clyde McPhatter and Ben E. King – among their ranks, their biggest and most enduring hits were made with vocalists who were little more than journeymen. Ultimately, what truly made the various incarnations of the group so great was that from their inception they were blessed with some truly great songwriters, arrangers and producers. The three-CD box **Rockin' and Driftin': The Drifters Box** is the only package to feature all their various incarnations and it includes their best work with Jesse Stone, the Erteguns, Jerry Wexler, Leiber & Stoller, Doc Pomus and Mort Schuman.

The group's domination of the R&B charts for the better part of a decade began in 1953, when Clyde McPhatter left the Dominoes and was signed by Atlantic's Ahmet Ertegun. McPhatter was a tenor blessed with an angelic voice and pin-up looks who, in combination with Bill Pinkney and Andrew and Gerhart Thrasher, took the Drifters to an R&B #1 with their very first single, Money Honey. While "Money Honey" is often cited as one of the "first rock'n'roll records", it is also a clear ancestor of soul. Written by Jesse Stone, the song is concerned with the realities of living in a material world and, though comic in tone, is an obvious forerunner of records by Barrett Strong, the Silhouettes, Otis Redding, Gwen Guthrie and countless others. In McPhatter's vocals you can clearly hear Jackie Wilson coming down the road. McPhatter's gospelesque flights of fancy continued to produce hits like **Honey Love, Such a Night** and **What'cha Gonna Do**, but at the end of 1954 he left the group to pursue a solo career.

That the Drifters continued to have hits after McPhatter left was largely due to the production of Jerry Wexler and Ahmet and Nesuhi Ertegun and musicians like saxophonist Sam "The Man" Taylor, guitarist Mickey Baker and drummer Panama Francis. With the smoother, less nasal (and less distinctive) Johnny Moore taking over as lead, the Drifters had hits with **Adorable, Steamboat, Ruby Baby** and **Your Promise to Be Mine**, but after 1956 the group was plagued with line-up changes and infighting, and in 1958 the entire group was sacked by their manager, George Treadwell.

With gigs scheduled at the Apollo Theatre, Treadwell found a local group called the Crowns to become the new version of the Drifters. Led by Ben E. King, their debut recording, 1959's **There Goes My Baby**, is one of the most significant records in R&B/soul history. Produced by Jerry Leiber and Mike Stoller, "There Goes My Baby" was the first R&B record to feature strings, but more importantly it was the first record to elevate studio alchemy above a more natural sound, and in the process it moved R&B groups away from both the street corner and the church towards what would become known as soul. The song's vaguely Latin feel would become rather more pronounced on both **This Magic Moment** and **Save the Last Dance for Me**. King left the Drifters in 1960 and was replaced by Rudy Lewis and, once again, Johnny Moore. The hits didn't stop, though, and in **On Broadway, Up on the Roof** and **Under the Boardwalk**, the Drifters – with some help from Leiber & Stoller, Phil Spector, Bert Berns, Gerry Goffin and Carole King – continued to make heaven a place on earth.

⮑We almost chose **All-Time Greatest Hits & More: 1959–1965**, Rhino, 1988

23

Dyke & the Blazers

Funky Broadway: The Very Best of Dyke & the Blazers

Collectables, 1999

When it comes to sheer "unnnhhh", James Brown has only one rival, Arlester "Dyke" Christian. Knowing that his primal funk grunt transcended all language, Dyke even titled one of his songs "Uhh", and in Dyke & the Blazers he fronted what is probably the greasiest, *stankin'*-est band ever. Born in Buffalo, New York, in 1943, Dyke joined a local soul troupe called Carl LaRue and His Crew in the early '60s. Taken under the wing of Ohio DJ Eddie O'Jay (who was responsible for kickstarting the career of the O'Jays), LaRue and crew moved to Phoenix, Arizona, in 1964 to work with O'Jay, but disbanded after only a year.

Dyke stayed in Phoenix, where he formed the Blazers with himself on vocals and bass, Alvester "Pig" Jacobs on guitar, organist Richard Cason, drummer Rodney Brown and saxophonists Bernard Williams and J.V. Hunt. In 1966 the group recorded their first single, **Funky Broadway (Parts 1 and 2)**, for a local label called Artco. With its combination of Brownian motion on the bottom end and Stax grease on top, "Funky Broadway" was an immediate regional hit that attracted the attention of LA label Original Sound. With national distribution, this incredibly primitive slab of wax reached #65 on the pop charts and stayed on the R&B chart for six months. "Funky Broadway" was the first pop song with "funk" in its title and it was a harbinger of the revolution in black music – even James

Brown would have to wait another year to come up with a record as *nastay* as this.

After another R&B hit, the extremely fonky, but admittedly messy, So Sharp, the group hit the road – the presence of new bassist Alvin Battle allowing Dyke to slide, shimmy and drop to his knees during performances. 1968's Funky Walk (Parts 1 and 2) began with a guitar line that presaged Led Zeppelin's "Whole Lotta Love" and bumped and strutted its way to the R&B Top 30 with some of the meanest JB-style drums and chicken-scratch guitar riffs this side of Clyde Stubblefield and Jimmy Nolen. As the record faded out, Dyke paid extravagant tribute to Wilson Pickett, as well as Jimmy Smith and James Brown – a move that would presage the group's next big hit, 1969's We Got More Soul.

"We Got More Soul" was a typically sparse funk vamp so crude that Motown's producers probably held their noses whenever it came on the radio. Listing African-American musicians like Ray Charles, James Brown, Johnnie Taylor and Aretha Franklin, "We Got More Soul" was a black pride anthem as only Dyke could do it – it was even open-minded enough to give a shout to supper-club chanteuse Nancy Wilson and, umm, Pearl Bailey. "We Got More Soul" sneaked into the pop Top 40, but their biggest hit was probably the follow-up, Let a Woman Be a Woman, Let a Man Be a Man. Another cryptic political ditty, "Let a Woman …" was a Top 5 R&B smash and has one of *the* great breakbeats, which has featured on countless records ever since.

Dyke & the Blazers released only a few more singles, including an outrageous cover of You Are My Sunshine and the string-soaked, Norman Whitfield rip-off, Runaway People. By early 1971, funk seemed to be getting too sophisticated for a musician like Dyke and he never got the chance to develop in a different direction. On March 30, 1971 he was shot outside a bar in Phoenix and his killer has yet to be tried.

⊃ We almost chose **So Sharp!**, Kent, 1991

24

Earth Wind & Fire

Greatest Hits

Sony Legacy, 1998

If funk was a TV programme, then George Clinton's P-Funk Thang would have been the evil twin of Earth Wind & Fire's clean-cut hero. Where P-Funk had mad-scientist plans to conquer the world, EW&F played by the rules; where P-Funk read comic books and watched sci-fi flicks, EW&F read African textbooks and listened to motivational tapes; where P-Funk sang about sex and the evil that men do, EW&F sang about love and spirituality; where P-Funk played only vamps and grooves, EW&F played traditional, radio-friendly songs. Unsurprisingly, EW&F were the most commercially successful black group of the 1970s.

Earth Wind & Fire was the brainchild of Maurice White. White had worked as a session drummer for the fabled Chicago label, Chess, and as part of Ramsey Lewis's band before starting his own band in the early '70s. With brother Verdine on bass, an early incarnation of EW&F was responsible for the soundtrack for Melvin Van Peebles' original blaxploitation movie *Sweet Sweetback's Baadasss Song*, and also released a couple of so-so albums. After meeting falsetto singer Philip Bailey on tour in Colorado, Denver White decided to reorganise the band around him. Recruiting keyboardist Larry Dunn and saxophonist Andrew Woolfolk from Bailey's band, as well as guitarist Al McKay from the Watts 103rd Street Rhythm Band, and Johnny Graham from the Friends of Distinction, the White brothers started EW&F Mark II.

Their fourth album, *Open Our Eyes*, was the group's breakthrough. The album's two singles, Mighty Mighty and

Kalimba Story were fairly standard funk tracks but with lyrics couched in vaguely mystical, Afro-centric metaphors. The Egyptology gave the band their signature shtick, but it was their optimism that made them a commercial juggernaut. "Mighty Mighty" and "Kalimba Story" were both Top 10 R&B hits and made some noise on the pop charts. By the time of their next album, *That's the Way of the World*, EW&F were superstars. Riding a nasty chicken-scratch guitar lick, the self-actualisation lyrics of **Shining Star** worked so well that it reached the summit of the pop chart. The mellower, Philip Bailey-showcase title track followed and stalled just outside the Top 10.

More saccharine lyrics followed in the form of **Sing a Song**, but the groove was so sweet and uplifting that even the most hardened of cynics couldn't ignore it. Judging by its Top 5 chart position, they didn't. **Saturday Nite** and **Getaway** were similarly galvanising grooves, but their lyrics didn't make you cringe. Featuring two of EW&F's best singles, **Serpentine Fire** and **Fantasy**, 1977's *All 'N All* album was their best yet. "Serpentine Fire" was just as its title said – a sinuous bass-line wrapping itself around slithering guitar licks – while "Fantasy", with its Burt Bacharach-like horns, soaring strings and seriously funky bass-line and guitar riff, was pure pop bliss (that it only made #32 is stunning). With its popping rhythms, zinging horns and Bailey's angelic chorus, **September** was even more perfect than "Fantasy" and made the Top 10.

Not even disco could put a stop EW&F's hits. Teaming up with Philly girl group the Emotions, EW&F created one of the most enduring records of dance-floor escapism, **Boogie Wonderland**. They even managed to score their second biggest hit with a ballad in the age of the beat that never stopped. **After the Love Has Gone** would become one of the most influential ballads of the decade. By the turn of the '80s, however, the group couldn't keep up with the changing shape of R&B. Their last significant hit, **Let's Groove**, was a magical pairing of Bailey's falsetto and a flatulent synth-bass riff.

⭢We almost chose **All 'N All**, Sony, 1977

25

Missy "Misdemeanor" Elliott

Supa Dupa Fly

Elektra, 1997

Supa Dupa Fly producer Tim "Timbaland" Mosley is one of the most innovative R&B producers of the 1990s. One day, his collected works will serve as a crash course in the art of hi-tech production, but until that day *Supa Dupa Fly* will have to do. Granted, with his hyper-syncopated beats and almost surreal digital sheen, Timbaland may very well be a one-joke act, but his punch line was the single most influential sound in music at the end of the last millennium.

Like Teddy Riley before him, Timbaland has reunited the sonic spirit of hip-hop with the shiny material of R&B. While hip-hop has sounded as if it's been stuck in one of RZA's moody string loops for most of the '90s, Timbaland has recaptured its original anything-goes essence. With his unique sonic palette, this Virginian Björk fan has redefined the sound of R&B on records like Magoo & Timbaland's "Up Jumps Da Boogie" (skittering hi-hats, Gothic synth-string stabs and liquid-mercury keyboards), Aaliyah's "Are You That Somebody?" (bionic human beatboxing, gurgling babies and a Swiss-cheese rhythm track), Whitney Houston's "It's Not Right, But It's OK" (making Whitney listenable) and Missy Elliott's *Supa Dupa Fly*.

Supa Dupa Fly's first track proper (after an intro from Busta Rhymes), **Hit 'Em Wit Da Hee**, features a sample of Björk's "Joga", video-game sounds from the Jamaican dancehall and one of the craziest guitar sounds you'll ever hear. Timbaland doesn't let up with the wild futurism for an instant and with

Supa Dupa Fly he created the blueprint for late '90s dance music. As Mosley and his assembled crew of rappers and singers are so fond of pointing out, everyone – from any R&B act that gets anywhere near the charts to British house producers Basement Jaxx – has stolen his beats. While Timbaland has the most recognisable aural signature since Holland-Dozier-Holland, even his throwaways don't sound repetitive. Beep Me 911 is an object lesson in how to stay fresh and how to show up the beat-biters. From the guy imitating a syn-drum with his mouth in the background, to the angelic choir buried in the mix, "Beep Me 911" is a modern version of Phil Spector's wall of sound that manages to stay just on the right side of overload.

Having Missy Elliott front your best productions hasn't hurt, of course. Misdemeanor is the closest thing R&B's had to an iconic presence since Prince and Michael Jackson fell off. With the exception of Mary J. Blige and Lauryn Hill, just about every other female R&B act is putty in the producer's hands. Elliott, on the other hand, is clearly her own woman. Showing why hip-hop has more or less killed off soul music, Elliott is pure attitude. She wouldn't be welcome in most hip-hop ciphers, but she's upfront and right there in your face in an age when no one but the fiercest gangsta rapper has got any 'tude to speak of.

With a bold supahero up front and a brainy producer behind her, Misdemeanor and Timbaland is a tag team that could compete with the Road Warriors and the Freebirds. Their submission hold is the track that made Missy a star, The Rain (Supa Dupa Fly). With a sample of the weirdest R&B track until Timbaland came along, Ann Peebles' "I Can't Stand the Rain", a freaky, off-kilter bass-line and Missy rapping lines like, "Beep, beep, who's got the keys to the jeep/Vrrrroom", "The Rain" was the most crunching calling card since Ric Flair's figure-four leg lock.

⮌We almost chose **Da Real World**, Elektra, 1999

26

En Vogue

Funky Divas

EastWest, 1992

The late 1980s and early '90s were not a good time for soul/R&B. Teddy Riley's New Jack Swing mixture of hip-hop and soul had opened the flood-gates for a whole heap of smarmy lovemen who had more self-regard than ability, and this deluge of glorified Chippendales caused hip-hop crews like De La Soul to refer to R&B as "rap and bull-shit". With the spectres of Mariah Carey and Whitney Houston looming over everything, female artists weren't offering much of a reprieve either. Then came En Vogue. They may have been no less the product of Svengalis than the Boys or Another Bad Creation; they may have been as cynically MTV-friendly as TLC and used beats as tired as MC Hammer; but no other artists of the era did pop-soul as well as they did.

The En Vogue concept was masterminded by producers Denzil Foster and Thomas McElroy (who also worked with Tony Toni Toné). Foster and McElroy had previously been responsible for Club Nouveau's pop #1 cover of Bill Withers' "Lean On Me" in 1987 and this crossover savvy came to the fore with En Vogue. The group was formed in Oakland, California at an audition in 1988, for which Cindy Herron, Dawn Robinson, Maxine Jones, Terry Ellis and one other singer showed up. The other singer was ruled out and 4-U was born. They soon changed their name to Vogue and then En Vogue, appearing on Foster and McElroy's *FM2* album in 1989. The group's first album, *Born to Sing*, featured the brilliant sin-gles "Hold On" and "Lies", but little else of interest. 1992's

Funky Divas was a more fully realised affair, although you still had to fast-forward through the painful cover of the Beatles' Yesterday.

Designed as a group that appealed to both men and women, part of En Vogue's success can be attributed to the fact that they seemed to be less of a constructed male fantasy than most of their girl-group ancestors. It's hard to imagine another female harmony group (aside from perhaps TLC) singing a song as political as **Free Your Mind** or a song as tough as **My Lovin' (You're Never Gonna Get It)**. Foster and McElroy also dared to employ arrangements as varied as the rock guitars of "Free Your Mind", the grinding James Brown funk of "My Lovin'", the supper-club jazz of **Giving Him Something He Can Feel** and the po-mo exotica of **Desire**.

The other big reason for the group's success was their videos, and it's impossible to listen to *Funky Divas* without picturing them strutting their funky stuff on the catwalk in their futuristic LaBelle outfits or crooning to an audience of sweating men in their crushed red velvet get-ups. It wasn't just that they looked damn good, but that their videos created the blueprint for all subsequent diva clips: that almost digital blue lighting, the stretched film, the high contrasts, etc.

Luckily, Foster and McElroy were as talented as the make-up artists and the musical language as strong as the visual language, creating a pop-soul vernacular that would become widespread over the next few years: "My Lovin'" was largely a remake of "Hold On", with even more hooks and horn stabs that would launch a hundred other records; "Free Your Mind" borrowed ideas from both George Clinton and Michael Jackson's "Beat It", as it predated the inevitable rap–rock fusion at the end of the decade; "Giving Him Something He Can Feel" was a verbatim reading of Aretha Franklin's 1976 version that must have given Puff Daddy an idea or two. Yet however many second-wave girl groups follow in their wake, none of them seem to be able to get it together as well as En Vogue.

⊃We almost chose **Born to Sing**, Atlantic, 1991

The "5" Royales

All Righty! – The Apollo Recordings

Westside, 1999

Perhaps more than any other vocal group, the "5" Royales epitomise the prehistory of soul music. The roots of the "5" Royales lay in a gospel group, the Royal Sons, which was formed by Lowman Pauling, Clarence Pauling, Windsor King, William Samuels and Anthony Price in Winston-Salem, North Carolina, in 1938. In 1951 the group (with entirely new personnel except for Lowman Pauling) recorded two singles for the New York-based Apollo label ("Bedside of a Neighbour"/"Journey's End" and "Come Over Here"/"Let Nothing Separate Me") in the style of the Soul Stirrers. By the end of 1951, the group had moved to New York, where Apollo began recording them as a secular group.

Compared to the Royal Sons' gospel recordings, which were raggedy, rough and sung over primitive instrumentation, the newly minted "5" Royales sounded smooth and polished. For their first single, Too Much of a Little Bit/Give Me One More Chance, the line-up included Pauling, Johnny Tanner, Jimmy Moore, Obadiah Carter and Otto Jeffries. Recorded in 1951 and released the following year, "Give Me One More Chance" could very well be the Rosetta Stone of soul. Even more obviously than Billy Ward & the Dominoes' "Have Mercy Baby" and "Sixty Minute Man", "Give Me One More Chance" was a secular lyric sung with a holy feel. Over an instrumental backing which was pure devil's music, the "5" Royales crooned like angels with the odd flourish borrowed from the Orioles.

The group's big commercial breakthrough came with Baby, Don't Do It in 1953. With its rollicking R&B backing and gospel soars, whoops and pleads, "Baby, Don't Do It" was a #1 R&B hit and started a chart run of five Top 10 R&B hits over the next year. By this time, Eugene Tanner had replaced Jeffries to form the classic "5" Royales line-up. Even bigger than "Baby, Don't Do It" was their two-sided smash, Crazy, Crazy, Crazy/Help Me Somebody, which also hit #1 in 1953. The single was everything '50s R&B was about: one side ("Crazy, Crazy, Crazy") was all honking saxophone, rolling piano, relaxed vocals and throwaway jive, while the flip was a gospel testifying of very secular blues.

With the exception of Laundromat Blues, all of the "5" Royales' hits were written by Lowman Pauling, and his standing as one of the truly great R&B songwriters would come to the fore when the group moved to King in 1955. Pauling's stinging guitar style would also become prominent on their King recordings and exert a huge influence on Stax guitarist Steve Cropper and on the British blues movement. Despite their success with Apollo, the "5" Royales wouldn't hit the charts again until 1957. Laden with guitar reverb, Holy Roller handclaps and one of Johnny Tanner's best performances which set the stage for Bobby "Blue" Bland, "Think" was the finest record of their career. They followed it up with "Dedicated to the One I Love", in which Tanner's lead connected together the entire prehistory of soul, from the blues to gospel.

Unfortunately, it fell to other artists to spark public appreciation of the "5" Royales' King material. "Think", "Dedicated to the One I Love" and "Tell the Truth" all became bigger hits for James Brown, the Shirelles, the Mamas & Papas and Ray Charles. Meanwhile, unique Pauling compositions like "Monkey Hips and Rice" and "Slummer the Slum" were completely ignored and the "5" Royales gradually faded into oblivion.

⮷We almost chose **Monkey Hips and Rice**, Rhino, 1994

28

The Four Tops

The Ultimate Collection

Motown, 1998

One of the great fallacies surrounding soul music (perpetrated by both aficionados and philistines) is that Motown is a diluted version of black music. It's a patently racist assumption, but you can almost see what they're getting at: the deportment lessons, the strings and celestes, the sing-song melodies, the blind crossover ambition. They may even have a point with the Supremes, but how on earth do these nay-sayers explain the Four Tops? With arrangements based around rhythms developed from prayer-meeting handclaps and tambourines and the Pentecostal bluster of lead singer Levi Stubbs, the Four Tops were the most gospel-grounded Motown act. For all the sweetened production Holland-Dozier-Holland might have layered on, and for all the supper-club blandness of backing vocalists Renaldo "Obie" Benson, Abdul "Duke" Fakir and Lawrence Payton, Stubbs' testifying of the torment of love never let the group leave the gospel firmament for the purgatory of pop.

The Four Tops formed in Detroit in 1953 and recorded largely unnoteworthy material for several local labels before joining Motown in 1963. Paired with producers/songwriters Brian Holland, Lamont Dozier and Eddie Holland, the Four Tops first made their mark with 1964's Baby I Need Your Loving. While H-D-H became famous for their work with the Supremes, their records with the Four Tops made them perhaps popular music's greatest production team. "Baby I Need Your Loving" has all of their familiar elements: the urgent, tumbling rhythm and overwhelming brass charts mirroring Stubbs' anguish matched with a simple, cheery melody and finger pops, suggesting that all is not doom and gloom.

The Tops' follow-up hit was **Ask the Lonely**, produced by Ivy Hunter and William Stevenson, but it was their next single that made the group superstars. 1965's **I Can't Help Myself** remains perhaps the definitive pop single: no matter how much you resist its almost irritating rhythm, cheesy saxophone solo and relentlessly corny "Sugar pie, honey bunch" refrain, "I Can't Help Myself" evades your defences and crawls under your skin. The record was so effective (it was an American #1) that the follow-up was exactly what it said it was, **It's the Same Old Song**, and reached the American Top 5.

The Four Tops and H-D-H hit their peak with their second #1 single, **Reach Out I'll Be There**. Forget Phil Spector, this was the real "wall of sound": Grand Canyon echo, eerie flute melody, surging drums, seismic bass, galloping percussion, the guttural "hah" that punctuates the dramatic pauses and, most of all, Stubbs' overwhelming voice.

The clip-clop rhythm from "Reach Out" continued on **Standing in the Shadows of Love**, another masterpiece of towering emotion, this time carried by the insistent percussion which would soon become the hallmark of Norman Whitfield's productions with the Temptations and, by extension, disco. **Bernadette** completed this trilogy of outstanding singles, which established the blueprint for the paranoid soul that would mark the end of the '60s and the early '70s. On "Bernadette", released in February 1967, H-D-H took all of the Motown conventions – liquid bass-line, pounding drums, strings, saccharine choruses – and rearranged their pop affirmations to make them downright scary.

After a couple of singles that followed the same path, but with less successful results, H-D-H left Motown, and the Four Tops were saddled with wretched material like "Walk Away Renee". They had hits through the '70s, but they never again reached the same heights as they did with Holland-Dozier-Holland.

⟲We almost chose **Anthology**, Motown, 1974

29

Aretha Franklin

Queen of Soul: The Very Best of Aretha Franklin

Rhino, 1994

As the daughter of one of America's most famous Pentecostal preachers, Aretha Franklin spent her childhood as a gospel singer with a remarkably precocious talent. In 1956, at the age of 14, she recorded a version of "Precious Lord" that heralded her arrival as one of the greatest singers of the twentieth century. Four years later, she moved to New York to become a pop singer and was signed by John Hammond to CBS/Columbia Records. Hammond, who was one of the major figures behind the blues revival of the '60s, was a died-in-the-wool purist, incapable of responding to the musical changes going on around him. He saw Franklin as the successor to Billie Holiday and tried to fashion her into a melancholy torch singer, with mixed results. Although the "standards" format showcased Franklin's protean talents as a pianist more obviously than her subsequent material would, her voice lumbered along with trite material like "Over the Rainbow" and "Love For Sale". She made some decent records at Columbia like her tribute to Dinah Washington, but while James Brown was belting out "Papa's Got a Brand New Bag" Franklin was shackled to material like "Misty" and "If I Had a Hammer".

In 1966 Atlantic bought Franklin's contract and paired her with producer Jerry Wexler. In January 1967, Wexler brought Franklin to Fame studios in Muscle Shoals, Alabama, where a white house band made the toughest soul music outside of Memphis. With guitarist Jimmy Johnson, organist Spooner Oldham, drummer Roger Hawkins, bassist Tommy Cogbill and guitarist Chips Moman creating a secular cathedral out of gospel elements, Franklin felt at home and produced the exquisite I Never Loved a Man (The Way I Love You), her first real hit and an R&B chart-topper for seven weeks.

With many of the same musicians in New York a month later, she came up with her towering achievement. Otis Redding would complain that Franklin stole Respect from him, but she did more than steal it, she made it completely her own. Evolving out of Aretha and her sister Carolyn fooling around in the studio, "Respect" may have been impromptu, but the details are so perfect they seem as if they've come from one of da Vinci's notebooks. The moment where Franklin breaks it down – "R-E-S-P-E-C-T" – is more than just an undeniable hook, it's also a stunningly effective political statement: "What, do I have to spell it out for you?"

While "Respect" was fixed atop the R&B charts for most of the summer of 1967, Franklin continued to record some of soul's most enduring records. Baby, I Love You, Chain of Fools, Since You've Been Gone (Sweet Sweet Baby) and Think had all raced to the top of the R&B chart by the summer of 1968, while (You Make Me Feel Like) A Natural Woman was kept from the top only by Sam & Dave's "Soul Man". It was a staggering run that made Franklin the undisputed "queen of soul".

With the exceptions of 1972's Day Dreaming and Rock Steady, Franklin's subsequent hits weren't as epochal as those of 1967 and 1968. They were merely the sound of the world's greatest voice relaxing and doing stuff that turned her, or her producer, on. Although it doesn't have any of her gospel recordings, this distillation of Rhino's four-CD box set has pretty much the best of her Atlantic years and is the best single-disc collection currently available.

⊃We almost chose **Queen of Soul: The Atlantic Recordings**, Rhino, 1993

Funkadelic

Maggot Brain

Westbound, 1971

It's safe to say that nobody has traversed the mind–booty divide more audaciously than George Clinton's Parliafunkadelicment Thang. With an unhealthy interest in scatology, Clinton attempted to solve Western philosophy's mind–body problem by merging the alternate universes he found in effluence, coitus, black radio, conspiracy theory, comic books, nursery rhymes and advertising slogans with the close-harmony singing, transcendence and physicality of the gospel tradition. With his equation of headspace and dance floor, Clinton demonstrated that black music was only capable of expressing the urges of the body as the racist fallacy that it was.

While the future Dr. Funkenstein began his musical life as the leader of a doo-wop band called the Parliaments in New Jersey in 1956, the P-Funk experience didn't take shape until Clinton took the group to Detroit in the '60s with the hope of getting signed to Motown. Berry Gordy passed on the group, but signed Clinton as a songwriter/producer. Clinton spent most of his time, however, moonlighting for local Motown rivals like Revilot, Solid Hit and Groovesville where, working with Andrew "Mike" Terry and Sidney Barnes as Geo-Si-Mik, he produced and wrote several Northern Soul gems for Darrell Banks, J.J. Barnes and the Debonaires.

The Parliaments' 1967 Revilot single, "(I Wanna) Testify", was the genesis of Clinton's blend of psychedelia and vocal group harmonising. Predating both Sly Stone's "Whole New Thing" and Norman Whitfield's more experimental productions for the

Temptations and the Undisputed Truth, "Testify" reached the American Top 20 on the back of its prescient, guitar-led blue-print for soul's hippy crossover success. Soon afterwards, Clinton would start dropping acid, grooving to the MC5 and digging John Sinclair's sexual liberation = political freedom spiel. With the addition of the hard funk bottom from Sly Stone and James Brown and Jimi Hendrix's freak-outs, the strands of Clinton's twisted vision coalesced and were expressed to their fullest on Funkadelic's (originally, the Parliaments' backing band) 1971 album, **Maggot Brain**.

Maggot Brain was as bleak as Sly Stone's *There's a Riot Goin' On*, as washed-out as the Rolling Stones' *Exile on Main Street* and as aggressive as Black Sabbath's *Paranoid*. As soul and funk were turning their backs on crossover success and looking inwards, Funkadelic had its eye firmly on "white" rock and pro-duced music more attuned to the realities of black life than any of their contemporaries.

Wars of Armageddon took John Lennon's tape loops into the ghetto, while **Super Stupid** was (and is) the greatest heavy metal song ever. The result of Clinton directing Eddie Hazel to play like his "mother had just died", the title track was ten min-utes of devastatingly emotive post-Hendrix guitar primal scream-ing. Despite the band's proximity to the worst aspects of LSD excess and '60s libertarianism, even a hippy platitude like **You & Your Folks, Me & My Folks** was rescued by Clinton's unhinged imagination and Worrell's astounding McCoy Tyner-ish blocks of sound. **Can You Get to That** referenced the Beatles while joining the discreet conversation that soul was hav-ing about political betrayal under the guise of break-up songs; the bitingly sarcastic approach of **Back in Our Minds** predated the O'Jays' "Backstabbers" and "Don't Call Me Brother" in its attack on false brotherhood sentiments. The album's opening lines said it best: "I have tasted the maggots in the mind of the universe and I was not offended/For I knew I had to rise above it all or drown in my own shit".

⮑We almost chose **One Nation Under a Groove**, Warner, 1978

31

The Gap Band

The Best of the Gap Band

Mercury, 1995

Cameo may have had bigger hits and the Time may have spawned master producers Jam & Lewis, but the Gap Band were the quintessential funk band of the 1980s. From the sheen of their production values to their godawful ballads, these natives of Tulsa, Oklahoma epitomised funk's journey from the backwoods to the suburbs. More successfully than anyone else, the Gap Band managed to update the Parliafunkadelicment Thang sound for the Reagan era. In their hands, P-Funk's afronautic futurist soundworld was brought down to earth and became the sound of upward mobility and the comic-book narratives became boudoir poetry. While the brothers Wilson may have dumbed down George Clinton's vision, at their best they streamlined his complexity and made his sound more immediately booty-shaking.

Charlie Wilson and his brothers, Robert and Ronnie, began singing as choirboys in their father's church, but they had abandoned the Pentecostal melisma in favour of a slicker style by 1974, when the group recorded their first album, *Magician's Holiday*, for Okie rock star Leon Russell's Shelter label. The band's breakthrough would have to wait until they signed to Mercury and released *Gap Band II* in 1979. The album's two big hits, **Shake** and **I Don't Believe You Want to Get Up and Dance (Oops)**, were distillations of formulas created by the two biggest R&B bands of the time, P-Funk and Earth Wind & Fire. "Shake" was a barely reworked version of Maurice White's trademark jazziness, while "I Don't Believe

You Want to Get Up and Dance (Oops)" (aka "Oops Upside Your Head") borrowed the giggles, nursery rhymes and the lines, "The bigger the headache, the bigger the pill" and "It's funkin' habit forming" from P-Funk. It didn't do the group any harm, though, as "Oops" became a dance-floor sensation and hit the British Top 5.

The Gap Band started to stake their own turf with 1980's **Burn Rubber On Me (Why You Wanna Hurt Me)**, which became a #1 US R&B hit on the strength of Robert Wilson's crunching adaptation of Bernie Worrell's synth-bass-lines. Like all of the Gap Band's hits, "Burn Rubber" was produced by Lonnie Simmons at his Total Experience studio. Simmons was one of the main instigators of the synthification of '80s funk and one of his other glossy productions, Yarbrough & Peoples' "Don't Stop the Music", replaced "Burn Rubber" at the top of the R&B charts in February 1981.

Simmons and the Wilson brothers really dropped the bomb, though, with 1982's *Gap Band IV* album. Charlie's Stevie Wonder impression on "Stay With Me" made the group a favourite with the Luther Vandross crowd, while **Outstanding** became the ultimate MOR funk ballad. Once again, though, it was Simmons who dominated the track. His glistening production elevated "Outstanding" from sentimental schmaltz and his percussion hooks have enticed hip-hop producers to keep the song in the popular consciousness. **You Dropped a Bomb On Me** took "Burn Rubber"'s bass-line and magnified it a thousand times, but **Early in the Morning** was the track that catalysed the album's platinum success. Cruising on top of a similar synth-bass riff and an almost identical drum track to "Burn Rubber", "Early in the Morning" was the tale of the next day in the life of the jilted lover in "Burn Rubber".

The Gap Band would continue to have hits over the next couple of years, but by this point the synth-bass novelty had worn off and vocalists like Guy's Aaron Hall had stolen Charlie Wilson's fire.

➲We almost chose **Gap Gold: The Best of the Gap Band**, Polygram, 1985

32

Marvin Gaye

Anthology

Motown, 1995

Blessed with a gorgeous voice, impeccable phrasing bequeathed to him from his father's storefront church, and a square jaw and long lashes, Marvin Gaye was perhaps the quintessential pop star. He was an iconoclast who railed against both the machinery of stardom and social injustice – and, unlike other great pop stars, Gaye was also a peerless duet singer. His combination of arrogance and openness resulted in a staggering recorded legacy, superbly represented on this two-CD collection.

Gaye dropped out of high school in the mid-1950s to work with doo-wop legends Harvey & the Moonglows. The group's leader Harvey Fuqua brought Gaye to Detroit, where he met Berry Gordy and would join the Motown staff as a session drummer. Gaye's first Motown recordings were as a Nat "King" Cole-style balladeer, but they were hopelessly out of date. When he combined croon with rasp, though, the results were little short of magical. His first hits, 1962's **Stubborn Kind of Fellow** and **Hitch Hike**, featured some of the gutsiest vocals Motown would ever record.

While 1963's rollicking **Can I Get a Witness** continued to showcase Gaye's abilities as a secular gospel shouter, 1964's **How Sweet It Is (To Be Loved By You)** proved that Gaye could be just as effective by singing with seemingly effortless ease. After splendid records like **Ain't That Peculiar** and **I'll Be Doggone**, Gaye began his series of remarkable duets in 1966 with Kim Weston. Perhaps the slightest of all his duets, **It Takes Two** was nonetheless pure pop bliss summoned from one of Motown's most awkward arrangements. It was with Tammi Terrell, though, that Gaye would record his greatest duets. Helped in no small part by Harvey Fuqua and Johnny Bristol's dramatic arrangement, the soaring **Ain't No Mountain High Enough** (1967) began a string of epochal hits for the two that would include **Your Precious Love, If I Could Build My Whole World Around You** (both 1967), **Ain't Nothing Like the Real Thing** and **You're All I Need to Get By** (both 1968).

1968 was Gaye's year. Not only did he have monumental hits with Terrell, but he recorded one of the definitive soul singles, **I Heard it Through the Grapevine**. On top of mind-bogglingly detailed production from Norman Whitfield (including maybe the best strings ever to be featured on a pop record), Gaye delivered the opening salvo in the subgenre of paranoid soul that would characterise the best records of the next several years. As a follow-up, he released what most people consider to be the greatest soul album ever, 1971's *What's Going On* (four tracks are included here).

After *What's Going On* changed the shape and direction of pop music, Gaye retreated into his falsetto and framed it with sketchy but effective funk vamps on records like **You're the Man** and **Trouble Man**. In 1973 he emerged from his funk with the definitive quiet storm record, **Let's Get it On** – it was so sexy and such a great come-on that you could ignore lines like "We're all sensitive people".

After "Let's Get it On", however, Gaye's creative peak was over. He still emerged every so often, with sublime records like 1976's **I Want You** and 1977's **Got to Give it Up**, but by this point Gaye was in the process of divorce, owed millions to the tax man and was in a pharmacological haze. In the early '80s he moved to Belgium and released his last great single, "Sexual Healing" (not included here). Any comeback, however, was halted on April 1, 1984, when Gaye was murdered by his own father.

⊃We almost chose **Let's Get it On**, Motown, 1973

33

Marvin Gaye

What's Going On

Motown, 1971

Along with Stevie Wonder, Marvin Gaye was Motown's most versatile talent. Not only a great singer, his work with vocal group the Originals in the late 1960s proved that he was also a very capable writer and producer. At that time, however, the Motown organisation was at its most paranoid. Their star producers and songwriters, Holland-Dozier-Holland, had just quit the company to form their own label; Stax was nipping at their heels; and infighting and personal problems threatened the careers of some of the label's core artists. Gaye was always a bit rebellious and was never really comfortable with his pop image, so he was always treated with a little bit of suspicion by the company brass. There was little surprise, then, that when Gaye approached Motown head Berry Gordy with the idea of an entire album based around protest songs Gordy basically said: "Over my dead body."

While Gaye was battling for creative control over his career, he was further distancing himself from the label's quality control department by growing a beard and ditching the dapper suit. With his new threads and a socially aware attitude, in part precipitated by his brother's return from Vietnam, Gaye was seeking, like Sly Stone out in San Francisco, to unite the hippy vision of the world with the moral and stylistic authority of soul music. Despite Gordy's rebuff, Gaye went ahead and recorded **What's Going On** anyway. When he first heard it, Gordy allegedly called it "the worst thing I've ever heard in my life".

When it was finally released almost a year after it was recorded, *What's Going On* became a landmark in the history of pop music. From the voices and soprano sax that open the record to the use of multitracked vocals in which Gaye duets with himself, this album was unlike anything Motown had ever done before. Capitalising on the fact that many of Motown's session musicians were slumming jazz players, Gaye's arrangement was dense and complex, completely unlike the standard Motown beat – or, indeed, what anyone else was doing. Combining the stylistic innovations of Isaac Hayes' *Hot Buttered Soul* with the technological innovations of psychedelic rock, Gaye created a vision that united dystopia with hope. At the same time as he was chanting down Babylon, his gorgeous falsetto, the cocooning bass groove from James Jamerson, the gently percussive congas and the smooth horns all suggested that Eden was just around the corner if we could all just love each other. It might have been a platitude that not even someone like Melanie would have been comfortable voicing, but coming from a soulman that kind of "love" was a statement as powerful as anything Bob Dylan was conjuring up.

Soul's first concept album, *What's Going On* wasn't about the travails of an alienated rock star, instead it applied soul's great theme (love) and its cultural context (the gospel feel of the black church) to the real world. Previously, soul had channelled its rage, its frustration, its hope into love songs, but here, on the title track and on **Mercy Mercy Me (The Ecology)**, Gaye does the reverse. **Flyin' High (In the Friendly Sky)** takes the slogan of an airline and makes turning on, tuning in and dropping out a holy sacrament. The album almost ends with **Wholy Holy**, the most spiritual and optimistic track here, but Gaye knew that it would have made the album trite. Instead, it ends on **Inner City Blues (Make Me Wanna Holler)**, a tough, dramatic chain of catch-phrases that reads like graffiti, but, in Gaye's hands, becomes a staggering union of the blues and gospel that remains as potent today as it was then.

⟴We almost chose **Here My Dear**, Motown, 1978

34

Al Green

Call Me

Hi, 1973

More than any other performer of his generation, Al Green symbolises the secular/sacred divide that gives soul music its emotional power. Unlike many of his contemporaries, though, Green's attempt to have it both ways with God and sex is the product of intense, quiet introspection. Some have complained that Green is a solipsist, which may very well be true, but no one else has made such gorgeous music about being alone, and about wrestling with two very different kinds of joy.

Green's journey across the battlefield of sexual release and spiritual transcendence began in 1960, as a member of his brothers' gospel quartet, the Greene Brothers. After he was kicked out of the group when his father caught him listening to the worldly Jackie Wilson, Green tried his hand at pop music with the 1967 single "Back Up Train", which would become a US R&B Top 10 hit. When his next few releases failed to dent the charts, Green went to Memphis to record with producer Willie Mitchell. Mitchell's Hi Records had previously been known for some decent instrumentals and country records, but working with former Stax drummer Al Jackson, Jr., Green and Mitchell created the composite portrait of the soulman: both funky and forlorn, assertive and acquiescent, greedy and generous. The mixture would be so successful that Green would have 13 Top 40 singles between 1971 and 1976 and sell some 30 million records during the same period. Even more than Barry White or Teddy Pendergrass, Green would become the definitive '70s loveman. Where other soft-soul icons like Smokey Robinson, the Stylistics and the Delfonics were slightly wimpy and put-upon, Green's falsetto was just plain sexy.

Call Me is Green's masterpiece. A sad, painful, but ultimately uplifting exploration of loss, it displays the most generous view of love and sex ever voiced by a male singer. Green may be self-absorbed, but it's his openness that makes this such a great record: it is at once the best break-up, and the best make-out, record ever made. On **Call Me (Come Back Home)**, Green sounds simultaneously ragged and warm, like he was caught between an exasperated sigh and an affectionate whisper. Tailing Green's voice perfectly, Al Jackson's drumming sounds so simple, but no one has played the drums with as much finesse. He managed to make his kit sound driving and floating at the same time, a combination that gave Green's records their substantial bottom, but never overwhelmed his silky voice.

Have You Been Making Out O.K. is so intimate that you feel like you're standing next to the woman to whom he's whispering, while, with its explosive Memphis horns, **Here I Am (Come and Take Me)** is about as bawdy and salacious as Green would ever get ("But it don't take much for me before my cup runs over"). Elsewhere, his sensuous voice turns Willie Nelson's **Funny How Time Slips Away** from a cry-in-your-beer mourn to a warm embrace of good memories and Hank Williams' **I'm So Lonesome I Could Cry** into a gospel hymn. The album ends with **Jesus Is Waiting**, a track which acknowledged the spirituality in sexuality and the physicality of religious devotion.

In 1974, the year after *Call Me* was released, one of Green's former lovers threw a bowl of boiling-hot grits at him while he was in the shower and then killed herself. Although the incident eventually resulted in the nearly as brilliant **The Belle Album**, it also effectively ended Green's greatest period and his relationship with secular music.

⊃We almost chose **The Belle Album**, Hi, 1977

Guy

Guy

Uptown/MCA, 1988

Born in 1967, Teddy Riley is the most important figure in R&B of the past two decades. An accomplished multi-instrumentalist and a maestro of the sampler, it was Riley who, once and for all, took R&B out of the hands of the vocalist and put it into the hands of the producer: after him, the success of an R&B track was based almost entirely on the beats. Riley is often credited as the father of New Jack Swing – the combination of hip-hop and soul – and the reason that R&B and hip-hop were inseparable during the '90s. What is often overlooked, however, is that he had a hand in making hip-hop so attractive to R&B artists and producers in the first place: Riley was behind such classics as Doug E. Fresh's "The Show", Kool Moe Dee's "Go See the Doctor", Heavy D's "Mr. Big Stuff" and Rob Base & DJ E-Z Rock's "It Takes Two". Today's pop-rap figurehead, Sean "Puffy" Combs, actually carried Riley's keyboards around while he was an intern at Uptown Records and learned more than a trick or two from the master.

Despite his behind-the-scenes work on many of hip-hop's first significant pop successes, Guy was the project that really broke Riley. A trio of himself and brothers Aaron and Damion Hall, Guy permanently changed the face of R&B. Although traces of the church were still evident in his voice, lead vocalist Aaron Hall picked up where the Gap Band's Charlie Wilson left off, by situating soul firmly in a strictly secular uptown, with melisma that was as over the top as the band's leather suits.

While Hall, despite his he-man huskiness, unfortunately helped create the adenoidal whine that dominates R&B these days, Riley forged the angular beatscape that defines contemporary "urban" music.

With its synth hooks, glossy vocals and shiny production values, Guy's self-titled debut album was as upwardly mobile as anything by Luther Vandross or Anita Baker. Crucially, though, Guy were very much the product of the Harlem housing projects where they grew up and **Guy** never forgets the street. There are only two slow joints on the album; the rest of the tracks are uptempo funk jams that feature the crunching kick drums and smacking snares of mid-'80s hip-hop, but with the bounce of Cameo and the Gap Band. No one had ever achieved such a synthesis of the material good life with the vibes from the street, and every R&B producer from Dallas Austin to Rodney Jerkins has since tried to duplicate the Riley formula.

With the allusions to, and mutated samples of, Stevie Wonder, James Brown, Trouble Funk and the Mohawks, Riley didn't forget where he came from. However, Riley was a child of hip-hop and he chopped, edited and reconstructed the original soul groove so that it made sense to a generation whose fantasies were shaped by technology rather than the Church. The Riley sound is based on the interaction between the brittle beats of his armoury of drum machines and the plasmic brio of his synth bass. *Guy's* best tracks – 'Round and 'Round, Groove Me, Teddy's Jam and I Like – are collages of ricocheting kick drums, stuttering snares, backwards beats and screaming, farting, belching, crooning synths that turn the vocals into just another synth colour. It's this quality, however, that reveals the ultimate problem with the Riley sound: since Guy and Whitney Houston, R&B vocalists have aspired to a kind of digital linearity that mimics the cathedral of machinery in which they're placed, rather than aspiring to the dirt and grit of a church made of earth and wood.

⊃We almost chose **The Future**, Uptown/MCA, 1990

36

Isaac Hayes

Hot Buttered Soul

Stax, 1969

Often reduced to a caricature of a hyper-masculine black loveman, Isaac Hayes was in fact one of soul's most versatile talents. He was a session pianist at the Stax studios, where he played on sides by Otis Redding and Wilson Pickett; with David Porter he wrote classics like "Hold On! I'm Comin'", "When Something Is Wrong With My Baby", "Soul Man" and "B-A-B-Y"; and he scored the films *Shaft*, *Tough Guys* and *Truck Turner*. Above all, he was Stax's most successful artist – an amazing achievement considering the label had Redding, Sam & Dave, Booker T. & the MG's, the Staple Singers, Eddie Floyd and the Bar-Kays.

Hayes' first solo album, 1968's *Presenting Isaac Hayes*, was a commercial flop recorded in an impromptu trio format with MG's drummer Al Jackson, Jr. and bassist Donald "Duck" Dunn. To say that **Hot Buttered Soul** was a departure would be something of an understatement. Seemingly featuring a cast of thousands, with a battery of effects pedals, *Hot Buttered Soul* had only four songs and they averaged over eleven minutes each. Unlike the urgent gospelese declarations he wrote for Sam & Dave, Hayes' voice was deep, overwrought and thick as molasses. With even richer arrangements, an album has never been more appropriately named.

His soundtrack to *Shaft* may have the wah-wah riff of the gods, but *Hot Buttered Soul* was more influential. Just about all of '70s soul and disco owes a debt to this album – not to mention hip-hop. With its remarkable success – it simultaneously charted on

Billboard's R&B, jazz, pop and easy-listening charts and sold over a million copies, unheard of for an R&B album – *Hot Buttered Soul* single-handedly opened the doors for album-length statements by Marvin Gaye, Stevie Wonder, the O'Jays and Curtis Mayfield, while its production defined the sound of '70s soul by providing the blueprint for the likes of Philadelphia International, Barry White, Van McCoy and the Salsoul Orchestra.

The basic rhythm tracks for the album were created in one long session, with Hayes on piano and the Bar-Kays (bassist James Alexander, drummer Willie Hall and guitarist Michael Toles) providing the rhythm, while the strings were overdubbed in Detroit by arrangers Johnny Allen and Dale Warren after Hayes sang them the parts. The vision may have been Hayes', but it wouldn't have come together without the Bar-Kays and the visionary production by Al Bell, Marvell Thomas and Allen Jones.

The first few minutes of the first track, **Walk on By**, set the stage for the rest of the album and for the next decade: the organ and string intro was the blueprint for Willie Mitchell's productions for Al Green, the blazing wah-wah solo sounded like what Funkadelic were doing up in Detroit, the abstract keyboard noodling and angular guitar figures must have given Miles Davis an idea or two, and everyone stole the string stabs and loping bass shuffle. **Hyperbolicsyllabicsesquedalymistic** was an update of the hipster jive tradition started by Louis Jordan appended to a killer wah-wah groove, while **One Woman** was a cheating tale with sweetening straight out of the Nelson Riddle songbook. *Hot Buttered Soul*'s trademark cut, though, was Hayes' eighteen-minute-plus version of Jim Webb's **By the Time I Get to Phoenix**. Beginning life as a way of getting the crowd's attention in a nightclub, Hayes' eight-and-a-half-minute rap intro became his signature shtick and inspired the likes of Millie Jackson. Milking the song for all that it was worth, Hayes' vocals and the arrangement redefined the parameters of sweet soul and, just as he did with "Walk on By", deconstructed and recreated a pop standard.

⮑We almost chose **Shaft**, Stax, 1971

37

Lauryn Hill

The Miseducation of Lauryn Hill

Columbia, 1998

R&B circa 1997 was an ugly place to be. Sure, there was Missy Elliott and all that Timbaland ultra-futuristic, super-syncopated beat science. But for all of the changing production paradigms, the vocalists were still mirror-dancing prima donnas. Ever since the apotheosis of Luther Vandross, Whitney Houston and New Edition in the mid-'80s, narcissism had ruled R&B and threatened to fritter away all of the moral and aesthetic capital that soul had accumulated. With vocalists as self-involved as Mariah Carey, Ginuwine and Jodeci, opera divas had nothing on R&B singers in the vainglory stakes. Even supposed saviours like Maxwell and Erykah Badu didn't have much more to offer than decent voices, unconventional haircuts and Afro-centric wraps. In this climate, Lauryn Hill's first solo album was nothing short of a revelation.

Looking back to '60s and '70s soul's age-old virtues, referencing '70s sitcoms, reminiscing about mid-'80s hip-hop, dabbling in reggae and dancehall and digging in the crates like the best '90s beat-freaks, **The Miseducation of Lauryn Hill** was the black bohemian equivalent of a Beastie Boys album, but from a woman's point of view. Replacing the wisecracks and cheap laffs of the Beasties with a sense of personal triumph, Hill made the ultimate crossover album of the hip-hop era. It was impossible to make R&B this late in the '90s without engaging with hip-hop, but Hill's singular triumph was that by half-singing and half-rapping and by enveloping the album in a patina of Stax horns, fatback beats and Kingston, Jamaica voodoo, she managed to make hip-hop personal, to make it signify in the same way that vintage soul did, and that is why *The Miseducation of Lauryn Hill* deserves to be in this book.

Hill had come to prominence as a member of the Fugees, a hip-hop crew with Wyclef Jean and Pras Michel that had formed in New Jersey at the turn of the '90s. Their 1996 album, *The Score*, had been that year's big breakthrough on the strength of covers of Roberta Flack's "Killing Me Softly" and Bob Marley's "No Woman No Cry", which heavily featured Hill's sung vocals. Despite this success, the triumph of *The Miseducation of Lauryn Hill* still came as a shock. Written, produced and arranged largely by Hill, it was a slap in the face to everyone who thought that women in R&B were little more than blank slates with whom male producers worked their magic.

Although it began with Lost Ones, a tuff warning to any pretenders to the throne that L. Boogie already knew was hers, *The Miseducation* was a beacon of warmth in a landscape dominated by crude, hopeless hip-hop and crude, compassionless R&B. Even if tracks like Ex-Factor and I Used to Love Him were bitter break-up songs, the music and the overall feeling of the album were a warm antidote to the astringency and commercial gloss of so much black music of the decade. Borrowing catch phrases from *Welcome Back Kotter* and Steve "Silk" Hurley's "Jack Your Body", a melody from Grandmaster Flash and clavinet riffs from Stevie Wonder, Every Ghetto, Every City saw Hill biting into some coco-bread and remembering things past with a joy and a tenderness unheard of in this day and age. Everything Is Everything summarises the album's trick: like all the best soul, the soaring music – the string stabs, the upful drums, the motorvational scratches, the grain of her voice – transmits the album's message more potently than the lyrics, turning clichés into words that hit like the gospel truth.

⟳We almost chose **Angie Stone: Black Diamond**, Arista, 1999

38

The Impressions

The Very Best of The Impressions

Rhino, 1997

Although the Impressions never made the same kind of mark on mainstream America as Otis Redding, Aretha Franklin or Smokey Robinson, it would not be stretching it too far to claim them as the most influential of all soul vocal groups. With a hit-making career that ran from 1958 to the early '70s, only James Brown spent longer at the top during soul's golden age. Working with arranger/producer Johnny Pate, the group almost single-handedly created the blueprint for the softer sounds of Chicago soul, and did as much as anyone to secularise gospel.

The Impressions were formed in Chicago in 1957 by Mayfield, Jerry Butler, Sam Gooden and Arthur and Richard Brooks. Signed to Vee Jay, the group had their first hit with 1958's **For Your Precious Love**. With a lead vocal by Butler that was closer to a sermon than the mannered doo-wop-inspired vocals of the time, "For Your Precious Love" is yet another claimant to the title "first soul record". Though it reached #11 on the pop charts, the fact that the song was credited to "Jerry Butler & The Impressions" tore the band apart. Butler then launched a solo career, aided and abetted by Mayfield, who co-wrote, sang harmony and played "Pops" Staple-style guitar on the Top 10 hit **He Will Break Your Heart**. Ironically, the success of "He Will Break Your Heart" helped get the Impressions signed to ABC-Paramount in 1961. With Fred Cash replacing Butler, the Impressions' Drifters-influenced **Gypsy Woman** reached #20 on the *Billboard* chart.

The group's next breakthrough came in 1963 with **It's Alright** – their first record with Johnny Pate. With its horn charts, gentle propulsion, mellow harmonies and Mayfield's falsetto, "It's Alright" virtually wrote the Chicago soul rule book. It also began a two-year chart run that included such feel-good gems as **Talking About My Baby**, "I'm So Proud", **Amen** and **Woman's Got Soul**. Two of their best songs from this period, **Keep On Pushin'** and **People Get Ready**, rank among the very few soul records of the era to engage with the Civil Rights struggle. Combining the timeless imagery of black spirituals with heavenly harmonies and lush arrangements,"People Get Ready" and "Keep On Pushin'" remain great records not because of their righteousness, but because of their sublime craft.

By 1968, Mayfield was no longer couching his politics in churchy metaphors. **We're a Winner**, with its earthy lyrics and with its funkier bottom, set the new pattern. Although Mayfield's politics are little more than NAACP platitudes, in the context of soul's development they were shockingly radical. **This Is My Country** was one of the first soul songs to raise the subject of slavery, daringly staking a claim to American-ness on the grounds that the country was built on the back of "that peculiar institution". The #1 R&B hit, **Choice of Colors**, followed in a similar vein, while "Mighty Mighty (Spade & Whitey)" also staked out the same turf with a nod to Sly Stone.

1970's **Check Out Your Mind** was the Impressions' last hit with Mayfield as lead singer. As he left the group to devote more time to his solo career, Cash and Gooden recruited Leroy Hutson, and later Reggie Torian and Ralph Johnson, to replace Mayfield. The group went on to have a couple of successes, most notably "Are You Man Enough" from the *Shaft in Africa* soundtrack and the R&B #1 **Finally Got Myself Together (I'm a Changed Man)**, but by this time the group's best days were definitely behind them.

39

The Isley Brothers

It's Your Thing: The Story of the Isley Brothers

Sony Legacy, 1999

They may never be mentioned in the same breath as those titans of African-American music, Louis Armstrong and Ella Fitzgerald, but the Isley Brothers have maintained a career in the music biz for just about as long. Ever since 1957, when they released the mediocre doo-wop single, Angels Cried, the Isleys – in one form or another – have kept pace with changing styles and stalked the American R&B chart. But they have never really been innovators and are regarded, by some, as little more than survivors. This is unfair, and this excellent three-disc anthology shows that the group have been responsible for some of the most electrifying soul music ever recorded.

After recording a couple of more doo-wop singles under the supervision of *the* impresario of street-corner harmony, George Goldner, the Isleys – real-life brothers Ronald and Rudolph O'Kelly – were signed by RCA, who released their first hit, Shout. Recorded five years after Ray Charles' secular gospel megalith, "I've Got a Woman", 1959's "Shout" was pure Holy Roller dementia: over-the-top melisma, feverish handclaps, choral call and response, even the organist from the brothers' church. Aside from Ronald's falsetto "wooo", which launched a few dozen Beatles records, the most remarkable thing about this explosion of raw energy was that it was produced by those ham-fisted enemies of raw soul, Hugo & Luigi – the men responsible for chaining Sam Cooke to an army of strings.

Their next few singles were destroyed by Hugo & Luigi's routine suppression of swing, but when the Isleys moved to Wand

and recorded with producer Bert Berns they struck gold with Twist and Shout (famously covered by the Beatles) and the calypso-like original version of Who's That Lady. With the Stax label making soul funkier, the group decided to set up their own label, T-Neck. Realising that they needed a guitarist, Ronald discovered one James Hendrix playing in a bar in Harlem, and immediately gave him a starring role on their first T-Neck singles. The question of who influenced who immediately arises on the strutting Move Over and Let Me Dance (the vocals of which sound an awful lot like Jimi's) and the amazing gospel harmony–garage band soundclash, Testify.

After they failed to get any hits on T-Neck, the Isleys moved to Motown and had a major hit with the very Motownish This Old Heart of Mine. They weren't happy, however, and in 1969 left the label to reform T-Neck, inviting younger brothers Ernie and Marvin and Rudolph's brother-in-law, Chris Jasper, to join the group. This was the beginning of a new era of sartorial magnificence, with the group resplendent in fur-lined Elizabethan coats and velvet trousers. They changed their musical direction too, heralded by that masterpiece of funk, It's Your Thing, a song that began a string of *nastay* tracks like I Turned You On, Freedom, Keep on Doin' and the epochal Get Into Something (whose instrumental break would become one of the cornerstones of hip-hop).

While still maintaining a commitment to the funk, 1973's re-recording of "Who's That Lady" shined the spotlight on Ernie's post-Hendrix wah-wah guitar and highlighted the group's commitment to staying current. The Isleys started working with synth programmers and producers Malcolm Cecil and Robert Margouleff (who had previously assisted Stevie Wonder), and this partnership was responsible for the Mooged-out Fight the Power, Live It Up and Harvest for the World. In response to the quiet storm phenomenon of the time, the Isley Brothers covered their asses and became consummate purveyors of the saccharine ballad with a version of Summer Breeze and the original Between the Sheets.

↺We almost chose **The Isley Brothers Story Vol. 2**, Rhino, 1991

40

Jackson 5

The Ultimate Collection

Motown, 1996

From the Osmonds and the DeFranco Family to Boyzone and S Club 7, the Jackson 5 has inspired more bands, or rather more Svengalis, than the Beatles, the Rolling Stones and the Velvet Underground put together. Indeed, Michael Jackson's pre-pubescent vocal cords, his over-singing and his emulation of Diana Ross's streamlined style have done as much to undermine the gospel/ballad tradition of African-American singing as the more commonly blamed tendency of disco and funk to put beat before vocals. But for all his faults, the "King of Pop" still possesses more dynamism and charisma than any other performer this side of James Brown, and – alongside Prince – he's probably the best pure singer to emerge in the past three decades.

The Jackson 5's emergence could not have been better timed. With the rhythmic innovations of James Brown and Sly Stone, soul's emphasis was changing, its attitude becoming ever more assertive. By the end of 1969, Sly & the Family Stone was no longer the voice of a shiny, happy, integrated America. Sly turned to cataloguing the betrayals of the '60s dream and America needed a new black icon to make it feel good about itself. Instead of someone who still believed in the possibilities of the American experiment, this new icon was an 11-year-old boy who didn't know any better. The Jackson 5 were the first pop band of the '70s. With glam rock in the UK, the schlock shock antics of Kiss and Alice Cooper in the US, and the teenybop of the Osmonds and the Partridge Family, the pop of the first half of the '70s was all about running away from the '60s into the safe confines of a naive innocence. The Jackson 5 epitomised this retreat.

Paired with the Corporation – a team of producers that included Berry Gordy, Freddie Perren (who would later help to define mainstream disco with Yvonne Elliman, Peaches and Herb and the Sylvers), Deke Richards (Black Oak Arkansas) and Alphonso "Fonce" Mizell (responsible for records by Donald Byrd, Johnny Hammond, LTD and A Taste of Honey) – Jackie, Tito, Marlon, Jermaine and Michael rode in on streamlined Sly Stone rhythms and vivacious melodies to re-define pop music. Their first four singles – **I Want You Back**, **ABC**, **The Love You Save**, **I'll Be There** – all went to #1 in the US in less than a year, and only a spoilsport or a militant Maoist could deny that they were some of the greatest radio songs ever. Bursts of energy, syncopation, buzzing fuzz guitars, bridges stolen from the Meters, upful strings and intense lead vocals from Michael that sounded like he was singing for his life, the first three laid down the foundations not just for all subsequent teen pop, but for a good portion of '70s pop in general.

"I'll Be There" represents the bedrock upon which all teen pop is built. While Michael managed to transcend his age, the sickly arrangement and the icky concept of the Corporation to produce a more than competent ballad, paradoxically Jermaine, Michael's older brother, sounded like he didn't understand what the song was about. Innocence, confusion, cracking voices – it was puppy love personified and record producers the world over found a formula that they could exploit eternally.

After the group's first singles, it was a series of diminishing returns – check out their version of the Isley Brothers' "It's Your Thing". Apart from **Never Can Say Goodbye**, **Get it Together** and **Dancing Machine**, their ballads became so sick-ly that even prepubescent girls were probably turned off.

⊃We almost chose **Anthology**, Motown, 1986

41

Janet Jackson

Control

A&M, 1986

Only someone with a gargantuan ego could entitle their break-through album **Control** when it was little more than a production showcase for Jimmy Jam and Terry Lewis. Janet Jackson's songs (co-written with Jam and Lewis) helped to assert the youngest member of the Jackson clan's independence, but without the spiky beats, synth splinters and sharp bass-lines of Jam and Lewis, *Control* would have fallen as flat as her two previous albums of weak-as-water teen pop.

What Jackson did bring to the project was venom. Rebelling against her parents by marrying James DeBarge of DeBarge (the family harmony group that superseded the Jacksons at Motown), she was the only family member who seemed determined to make it in her own right. When her marriage failed six months later, instead of running back to her family she went to Minneapolis and recorded her third album with Jam and Lewis. As members of the Time, these two had been part of Prince's crew and had helped to redefine soul at the start of the 1980s. Since the group disbanded, they had become the hottest producers in R&B, crafting hits for the SOS Band, Cherrelle, Alexander O'Neal, Patti Austin and the Force MD's.

Many of the backing tracks for *Control* were actually already crafted by Jam and Lewis for an album they were working on with Atlantic Starr singer Sharon Bryant. She rejected the tracks, however, but when Janet Jackson showed up with her pissed-off lyrics, the tapes were recycled and the sound of '80s pop-funk was born. It's hard to imagine that the music wouldn't have had the same effect if Bryant had ended up singing, because Jackson, despite her appearances on TV shows like *Good Times*, *Facts of Life* and *Fame*, was hardly a star. It was *Control* that made her one.

Control would eventually sell some five million copies in the US, spawning one pop #1 and five R&B #1 singles. The album's first single, **What Have You Done For Me Lately** shook the foundations of an R&B world dominated at the time by Whitney Houston and Freddie Jackson. Lewis's drum programming leaped from the speakers, while Jam's ferocious bassline and angular synth riffs had an attitude, a strut, a funk that was wholly missing from the R&B records of the day. Until Teddy Riley (who was surely listening closely) came along, this was the closest R&B would get to hip-hop.

Nasty followed in quick succession with even bigger drums and Jackson's own keyboard line put together at such sharp angles that you could put your eye out if you listened too closely. Inspired by the work of New York disco producer John Robie with groups like C-Bank, the track was put together largely with the Ensoniq Mirage, the first sampling keyboard to hit the market. The track's jagged edges were pure Mirage; Jackson's toughest vocal ever only adds to the aggression. Featuring the most intricate drum programming (the result of sequencing mistakes), **Control** was the album's third, and last great, single.

By this time, the album was a commercial juggernaut, with **Let's Wait Awhile** and **The Pleasure Principle** reaching the top of the R&B charts and **When I Think of You** hitting #1 in the pop charts. They were all decent singles, but not as groundbreaking as the first three. Elsewhere, the stiff vocals and beats and plinky, new wave keyboards of **You Can Be Mine** serve to foreshadow Jam and Lewis's work with the Human League later in 1986. A rousing monument to the power of collaboration.

⊃We almost chose **Rhythm Nation 1814**, A&M, 1989

42

Mahalia Jackson

How I Got Over: The Apollo Sessions 1946–1954

Westside, 1998

For gospel aficionados Mahalia Jackson is merely one of a number of great singers. For the rest of the world, however, she is probably the only gospel singer they've ever heard of. This is largely due to her association with the Columbia label from the mid-1950s onwards and the high profile that the company's financial clout afforded her. Her greatness and her impact, however, stem from the recordings she made with the independent Apollo label in the '40s and '50s. Influenced by the two legendary Bessies – Johnson and Smith – Jackson brought a bluesy quality and an improvising gift to the stately manner of female gospel singing which in turn influenced practically every singer who came after her.

Appropriately for such a great synthesist, Mahalia Jackson was born in New Orleans. Though her parents were devout hymn-singing Baptists, she lived next to a Holy Roller church and incorporated their ecstatic shouting into her own style. Moving to Chicago in 1927, she joined the Johnson Singers (generally credited as the first professional gospel group) and began to fuse her Southern downhomeness with some Northern elegance, infuriating some congregations along the way with her suggestive movements. When the Johnson Singers broke up in the late '30s, Jackson recorded a couple of solo sides for Decca and then became a demo singer for the father of gospel music, Thomas A. Dorsey. With Dorsey she toured the US and established herself as one of the most famous singers on the circuit, the equal of other great gospel legends like Willie Mae Ford Smith and Sallie and Roberta Martin.

Move On Up a Little Higher, her third record for Apollo Records (for whom she signed in 1946), immediately became one of the biggest-selling gospel records of all time and it's not hard to see why: few performances captured on vinyl have quite such physical power as this does. It was followed, a year later, by the almost as bone-rattling **Dig a Little Deeper**, a release that marked the debut of Jackson's longtime pianist Mildred Falls. But while Jackson could rock'n'roll better than anyone, her potency on slow hymns like **Amazing Grace** and **Even Me** was diminished not a jot.

1950's **Just Over the Hill** was written by W. Herbert Brewster, the Memphis pastor who had written "Move On Up a Little Higher", and this became the second of her "going to heaven" trilogy. The final part was **How I Got Over**, on which Jackson roared so powerfully that the song eventually became a standard for the Civil Rights movement. Equally thrilling was her version of another Brewster composition, **These Are They**, in which she triumphantly overcame a production that made her sound like she was several hundred metres away from the microphone.

By the time the remarkable **I Bow On My Knees** was released in 1952, Jackson was a superstar. By this point, however, Apollo was backing her with male choirs, pushing her in a jazzier direction and providing her with less than worthwhile material. Nonetheless, her voice could overcome even the worst obstacles. On **Walking in Jerusalem** her squall eviscerates the jaunty male background choir, while on **I Wonder If I Will Ever Rest** her voice still sends shivers up the spine despite a wretched organ obbligato.

The arrangements became even stiffer and more pop-oriented following Jackson's move to Columbia in 1954, but this three-disc collection concentrates on her Apollo material and provides an apt testament for one of the greatest singers, secular or sacred, that the world has ever known.

⮱We almost chose **Gospels, Spirituals and Hymns**, Columbia, 1991

43

Michael Jackson

Thriller

Epic, 1982

As they used to say in the days of Elvis, 40 million **Thriller** buyers can't be wrong. There is a reason – besides hype – why this is the biggest-selling album of all time. Unlike other "event albums", like Peter Frampton's *Frampton Comes Alive*, Pink Floyd's *Dark Side of the Moon* or Alanis Morissette's *Jagged Little Pill*, where buying the thing along with umpteen million others was as much a part of the record's meaning as the music it contained, *Thriller*, along with the *Saturday Night Fever* soundtrack, is the only one that truly holds up long after the initial buzz has gone.

Thriller was straightforward pop's last gasp before Prince took it to the conceptual high ground and hip-hop dismantled its structure altogether. But it was more than just one of the most perfectly crafted albums ever made. *Thriller* was the culmination of the soul experiment: it was the ultimate crossover album and one of the best examples of white and black musicians working together to produce a unified vision. After *Thriller* both the R&B and pop charts, and the black and white underground scenes, veered away from each other and wouldn't meet up again until the sheer paucity of decent rock music made hip-hop's commercial victory inevitable. Perhaps this is why *Thriller* remains so vital – or maybe it's just the craft.

Even if it is just the craft, however, the implications of the way the album is put together are unavoidable. With its hard-rock guitar solo from Eddie Van Halen (which would become 1980s R&B's equivalent of country soul's black singer plus white session players formula), **Beat It** laid down the framework for the next two decades' worth of R&B integration. "Beat It" may have been nothing but the Rod Stewart/Rolling Stones disco moves in reverse, but it was the biggest blow to narrowcasting radio segregation of the '80s and laid the groundwork for Prince's crossover. **Wanna Be Startin' Somethin'** did start something by bringing the most underground aspects of disco into the mainstream. Stealing its hook ("Mamase mamasa, mama-makossa") from Manu Dibango's Cameroonian disco classic, "Soul Makossa", "Wanna Be Startin' Somethin'" highlighted both disco's integrationist ideal and its love of world music, thus giving the lie to disco's detractors by showing that it was more in tune to Africa than funk or any other form of "real" black music. The huge success of both **The Girl Is Mine** (recorded with Paul McCartney) and **Billie Jean** broke down MTV's colour barrier, forcing the network to play videos by African-American artists despite all of its costly market research and demographic projections.

While **Thriller** (particularly in its video form) and **P.Y.T. (Pretty Young Thing)** seemed to address, with some prescience, the image problems that would plague Jackson's career after *Thriller*, the most fascinating song here was "Billie Jean". Superficially a paternity saga of the sort that has occupied blues and soul since almost day one, in Jackson's hands "Billie Jean" became an interrogation of his past as an innocent child star who couldn't escape his image. With the virtuoso, moonwalking performances of the song on the Motown 25th anniversary TV special and on the video that would make him the Western world's biggest recording star, Jackson turned the song into an avowal of his sexuality. Of course, he wasn't very convincing and he sang "Billie Jean" like he didn't necessarily believe it himself and the abundant contradictions fascinated the entire world. After all, what is more mesmerising than to watch the mechanics of stardom unravel before your eyes?

⮐We almost chose **Off the Wall**, Epic, 1979

44

Louis Jordan

The Best of Louis Jordan

MCA, 1975

These days he may be remembered principally for providing the music for *Five Guys Named Moe*, but there was a time when Louis Jordan was so big that he duetted with Bing Crosby. Along with Nat "King" Cole, Louis Jordan was one of America's first crossover stars (he even had a #1 pop hit with G.I. Jive in 1944) and his easy-swinging hepcat jive numbers made the mainstream safe for the coming of rock'n'roll. Even more significantly, Louis Jordan and His Tympany Five were the most important R&B group of the '40s, not to mention the most successful R&B group of all time holding a never-to-be-broken record of 113 weeks atop *Billboard*'s "race chart".

Jordan was born in 1908 in a small town in Arkansas to a horn-playing father. Encouraged to play the clarinet at an early age, by the early '20s he was touring with the legendary Rabbit Foot Minstrels. By the time Jordan's family moved to Philadelphia in 1930, he had switched to alto sax and joined various jazz bands, culminating in a stint with Chick Webb's Savoy Ballroom Orchestra in 1936. After two years of playing second fiddle to Ella Fitzgerald, Jordan started his own group and landed a residency at Harlem's Elk's Rendezvous Lounge. The Elk's Rendezvous Band was a five-piece "jump" combo that played hot swing solos on top of shuffling boogie-woogie rhythms and this style was to dominate R&B for the next decade.

The band, renamed the Tympany Five in 1939, had their first hits in 1941 with I'm Going to Move to the Outskirts of

Town and **Knock Me a Kiss**. Over the next ten years, Jordan would reach the R&B charts a remarkable 57 times and between 1946 and 1947 he was at #1 for nearly a year and a half. While the jump style had various regional variations, Jordan, like Nat "King" Cole, had a geographically nonspecific singing style that appealed across the US. Also like Cole, Jordan exuded a suave cosmopolitanism and, despite his comedic songs, a distance that was closer to classic pop than the blues.

Like the calypso for which he had an affinity, however, Jordan's humour and detached air masked lyrics that were subtle protests against racism and injustice. **Beans and Corn Bread** was a Leiber & Stoller-esque quasi-novelty song about racial conflict, "Ration Blues" tackled poverty on the home front during World War II, and **Saturday Night Fish Fry** (Jordan's last big hit) was a diatribe against racist cops camouflaged as a party tune.

Jordan's greatest gift, though, was his sense of swing. As Jordan himself would've said, if songs like "Open the Door, Richard", "Ain't That Just Like a Woman" and **Ain't Nobody Here But Us Chickens** don't make you smile, then "Jack, You're Dead!". Far more than being mere commercial hacks, Jordan and the Tympany Five's blend of swing, humour and social commentary influenced nearly everyone who followed them. Jordan was James Brown's favourite artist, while Ray Charles recorded some of his songs and signed him to his Tangerine label in the '60s. Carl Hogan's guitar solo that introduces "Ain't That Just Like a Woman" was the influence for Chuck Berry's "Johnny B. Goode", while Jordan's squeals when he calls his lover girl in **Caldonia** set the stage for Little Richard. Even artists who could barely walk when Jordan was in his heyday found elements to borrow: you can definitely hear Junior Walker coming down the road in Jordan's sax solo on **Early in the Mornin'**.

⤷We almost chose **Let the Good Times Roll:
The Complete Decca Recordings**, Bear Family, 1992

45

Kid Creole & the Coconuts

Wise Guy (aka Tropical Gangsters)

Ze/Sire/Island, 1982

It wouldn't be much of a stretch to suggest that Tommy Browder (aka August Darnell and Kid Creole) is the greatest synthesist of disco, funk, salsa, Cab Calloway and Cole Porter the world has ever known. Just as his brother Stony tried to turn the ghetto into a glittering Broadway extravaganza with Dr. Buzzard's Original Savannah Band, Darnell suggested that style could transcend even the most brutal material reality. With their arch lyrics, Cotton Club horn charts, Great White Way vocal mannerisms, chicken-scratch guitars and bubbling bass-lines, Kid Creole & the Coconuts were simultaneously as fabulous as the Ziegfeld Follies and as abrasive as Johnny Rotten.

Paradoxically, the dawn of the Reagan/Thatcher era saw a convergence of black and white music that will probably never be seen again. Straddling New York's disco and new wave scenes, Kid Creole & the Coconuts adopted punk's main weapon – attitude – to compensate for their lack of roots and singing ability. Continuing from where Dr. Buzzard's left off, Darnell and co-conspirator Andy "Coati Mundi" Hernandez dressed themselves up in zoot suits, surrounded themselves with three hot backing singers, read from Bobby Short's supper-club lexicon and played confidence games with racial stereotypes.

Like their previous album, *Fresh Fruit in Foreign Places*, which found the entire world in the Big Apple's five boroughs, **Wise Guy** (or **Tropical Gangsters** in the UK) is a mock travelogue in which the band "are washed up on the shore of B'Dilli Bay – island of sinners ruled by outcasts where crime is the only passport and RACE MUSIC the only way out!" The pan-Caribbean vibe of *Fresh Fruit* reappears in the ersatz soca/salsa of **Annie, I'm Not Your Daddy**, the trade-wind lilt of **No Fish Today** and in the synthesised steel drum and timbale fills of **I'm Corrupt**, but mostly *Wise Guy* is straight-ahead, if slightly astringent, R&B. That is, as straight-ahead as can be expected from a guy who calls his backing musicians "The Pond Life Orchestra".

Even more than overorchestration, Darnell's main vice is his archness, but the directness of the music somehow manages to tone down his conceptual and lyrical excesses. "No Fish Today" is everything Steely Dan wanted to be but weren't: with the siren harps and sea-mist strings, the music evokes a tropical paradise which is undermined by one of the harshest dialogues this side of Harold Pinter, in which a fishmonger refuses to sell a woman fish during a shortage because "the authorities agree that if anyone should eat, it should be the upper class". Of course, the merchant is "neither right nor wrong, just another pawn" who "got to be this old because [he does] what [he's] told". More cruel still is the amazing "Annie, I'm Not Your Daddy". Over the most detailed music of his career, and with the Coconuts singing "onomatopoeia" in the background, Darnell doesn't break it to her gently: "If I was in your blood, you wouldn't be so ugly".

His music may be too knowing and his image too inauthentic ever to win mainstream acceptance, but you can't deny his singularity: only Darnell would have staged the break-up invective of **Loving You Made a Fool Out of Me** to Chic-meets-Ellington razzmatazz, or made a dance song about a **Stool Pigeon** ("The FBI rewarded him because they like a guy who will stab a friend"). Even when he plays the stereotypical stud, Darnell downplays it with humour: "Make you sure that you breathe before you break your back or get a heart attack."

⟳We almost chose **Fresh Fruit in Foreign Places**, Sire, 1981

46

Kool & the Gang

Wild and Peaceful

De-Lite, 1973

There is perhaps no greater compliment than being called "the second baddest out there" by James Brown. Before metamorphosing into purveyors of slick, smarmy pop hits in the late 1970s and early '80s, Kool & the Gang mined a deep, polyrhythmic, jazzy groove that was so innovative even the Godfather had to take notice. By the time of 1973's **Wild and Peaceful**, Brown wasn't just taking notice, he was running scared.

Beginning life as the Jazziacs in Jersey City, New Jersey, the band was founded in 1964 around bassist Robert "Kool" Bell and his multi-instrumentalist brother, Ronald (Khalis Bayyan). The Bells' father, Bobby, was a friend of Thelonious Monk and the boys were brought up with the sounds of Monk, John Coltrane and Horace Silver, which they took and blended with the rhythms of the street. With neighbours Dennis "Dee-Tee" Thomas (saxophone), Charles Smith (guitar), George Brown (drums), Robert "Spike" Mickens (trumpet), Ricky West (keyboards) and Woody Sparrow (guitar), the Jazziacs became the Soul Town Band, then the New Dimensions, then Kool & the Flames, and finally, when they signed to Gene Redd's De-Lite Records in 1969, Kool & the Gang.

The band's early records like "Chocolate Buttermilk" and "Let the Music Take Your Mind" showcased a sound that was heavily based on the Meters and Sly & the Family Stone – a combination of clipped guitars, bumping bass runs, lots of effects pedals and jazz chops. They had some moderate chart success, but it wasn't until 1973's *Wild and Peaceful* that they finally emerged with their own identity.

From Harlem to Times Square, the biggest record in New York in 1973 was Manu Dibango's "Soul Makossa". Recorded in Cameroon, "Soul Makossa" was a hypnotic rhythm-mantra that combined American funk and African polyrhythms. It was an enormous hit on both the funk and developing disco scenes and a hugely influential record. De-Lite wanted Kool & the Gang to do a cover version, but the band had their own ideas. Using "Soul Makossa" as a blueprint, they recorded the bulk of *Wild and Peaceful* in a single session. The album's first single, **Funky Stuff**, began with a party whistle and then settled into a bouncing groove that streamlined their previously meandering sound. "Funky Stuff" reached the R&B Top 5 and the pop Top 30, but the album's next two singles were even more successful. **Jungle Boogie**, again influenced by "Soul Makossa", had an impossibly tight, guitar figure fleshed out with a killer clavinet riff, Meters-style scat singing and Tarzan screaming. One of the out-and-out funkiest records ever, "Jungle Boogie" reached #2 and #4 on the R&B and pop charts respectively. Their first R&B chart-topper, **Hollywood Swinging**, borrowed the bass-line from another big record of 1973, Mandrill's "Fencewalk", appended to it to the band's first real "song" and truly established Kool & the Gang as one of the most commercially successful of all funk bands.

That was just the first side of *Wild and Peaceful*. The second featured extended jazz jams that the band crafted into message songs. **This Is You, This Is Me** featured lines like "Grow up in the ghetto, never seen a tree/If you don't understand the words to this song, it's on you, it's on me" over meditative, "spiritual" jazz licks, while **Heaven At Once** had the band claiming that they were "scientists of sound, mathematically puttin' it down". With its mixture of groove and message, the album spent a year on the album charts and became one of the pillars of funk.

↪We almost chose **The Best of Kool & the Gang 1969–1976**, Mercury, 1993

47

Little Willie John

Fever: The Best of Little Willie John

Rhino, 1993

If anyone invented soul singing, it was Little Willie John. There may have been gospel-influenced singers before, but none of them (and perhaps only James Brown since) sang with such intensity. And nobody has projected as much emotion, as much pure, abject misery as Little Willie John without becoming mawkish. John blended the crooning ballad style of Billy Eckstine and Nat "King" Cole with the naturalism of the blues, the physical impact of gospel and a bit of showbiz pizzazz. While some of his best records ooze an atmosphere of frustration and spent anger, he was also just about as sexy as it was legal to be in the 1950s. In short, he was the archetypal soulman.

Born William Edgar John in Arkansas in 1937, he moved to Detroit with his family in the '40s and in 1951 hooked up with the Johnny Otis Show. He spent much of the next few years moving in and out of bands, not staying long because of a wild streak and a street tough's version of the Napoleon complex. Hustling for work in New York, he was heard by Henry Glover of King Records, who signed him on the spot. Then, in June 1955, John recorded a version of a song that had just been released by Titus Turner. Turner's version of **All Around the World** was a novelty number that played the folkloric imagery as a joke, but that's not why no one has heard of Turner today. Along with Ray Charles' "I've Got a Woman" and Chuck Berry's "Johnny B. Goode", Little Willie John's version of "All Around the World" helped create the lexicon of release in popular music and blew Turner's version out of the water. Ignoring the comic element of the lyrics, John sings the song like he really means it: "All around the world, I'd rather be a fly/Alight on my baby, stay with her 'til I die/With a toothpick in my hand, I dig a ten foot ditch/And run through the jungle fighting lions with a switch".

If "All Around the World" (which reached #6 on the R&B charts) made John a presence on the scene, then his follow-up, Need Your Love So Bad, established him as one of the greatest singers ever to get on his knees in supplication. No soulman, not even Smokey Robinson, has ever sounded so miserable as John does here, but even when scraping the depths of despair John's performance is frighteningly intense. When he sings "Don't worry baby, we won't fuss and fight", the roots of James Brown's scorched-earth vocals on "Please, Please, Please" are apparent and, indeed, Brown went on to record a tribute album to Willie John following his death in 1968.

If John is known at all, though, it is for his original version of Fever, in which his increasingly hoarse excitement powerfully embodies the song's heated passion. "Fever" reached #24 on the pop charts and was later covered by Peggy Lee with her Mae West come-on routine, who ripped off the arrangement and John's phrasing note for note while failing even to approximate his vocal panache.

John continued to have pop successes with Talk to Me, Talk to Me, Leave My Kitten Alone and Let Them Talk, but the arrangements got progressively more string-soaked and pop-oriented. By the early '60s, he could still sing circles around anyone, but the hits stopped coming and he got increasingly irascible. In October 1964, he stabbed a man in a fight at a house party and was sentenced to eight to twenty years for manslaughter. On May 26, 1968, he died in prison in mysterious circumstances: pneumonia, the initial listed cause of death, was later changed to heart attack.

⮑We almost chose **Mister Little Willie John**, King, 1987

48

Teena Marie

Starchild

Epic, 1984

With her boudoir poetry, strained similes and overripe metaphors, Teena Marie's "opening line may be a bit passé", but no one, with the exception of Prince, so perfectly encapsulated the 1980s. **Starchild** is full of angular funk jams, shoulder-padded power ballads, Harold Faltermeyer synth arrangements, he-man guitar solos and the ultimate Reagan-era couplet: "Looking out the window I can hear an engine roar [cue revving noises]/Cobalt blue Pantera dashes through the garage door". Alright, so you may need to wear parachute pants or a Madonna bow to appreciate it fully, but *Starchild* is, nevertheless, one of the few '80s R&B albums to explore what gave soul its original dynamic thrust – the tension between the spirit and the flesh. But what the neon-lettered and airbrushed sleeve art makes clear is that Teena Marie's conception of spirituality goes a lot further than the biblical passages she cites more than once; there is also a lot of the unicorn-stickered otherworldliness of pre-adolescent girls on display here.

In the '80s R&B moved irrevocably out of the church and into the shopping mall, and Teena Marie was the ultimate transition artist. Beginning life in suburban Santa Monica, California in 1957 (as Mary Christine Brockert), she was signed to Motown in the late '70s and paired with Rick James, who moulded her into Motown's most successful white artist. After a string of R&B chart hits like "Behind the Groove" and "Square Biz", Marie left Motown in a dispute over royalties in 1983. *Starchild* was her first album with Epic and the most successful of her career. Ditching the slap-bass sound of James's Stone City band in favour of the processed guitars and synth curlicues of Minneapolis, Marie found the ideal vehicle for her slightly astringent vocal style.

Just like Prince, the architect of the Minneapolis sound, Marie was a multi-instrumentalist – as well as producing *Starchild* and writing and singing all the songs, she also plays guitar, piano, synth, drums, percussion and programmes the drum machines. Also like Prince, she attempted to have it both ways with sex and God. But where Prince is firmly convinced that paradise is earthly, Marie isn't sure. On **Help Youngblood Get to the Freaky Party**, an innocent churchgoer is accosted by a sweet-rapping Lothario and only just manages to hang on to her chastity even though the sultry guitar lets you know that she really wants him to bring the freak out in her. Elsewhere, though, the church has no hold on her. Instead of using gospel hosannas to give voice to her overwhelming passion, Marie writes flowery entries in her secret diary. Her lover doesn't take her to heaven, but beams her up to the Milky Way and transports her to ancient Egypt.

Arguably one of the principal legacies of disco was the decline of the classic soul ballad. Before disco, there wasn't too much of a drop-off in quality from fast songs to slow ones; after disco, it was endemic. Unfortunately, Marie is no exception and the slow numbers on **Starchild** are a major disappointment. The uptempo tracks, however, are what you pay the price of admission for: **Lovergirl** is the best non-Prince Prince song ever, "Help Youngblood Get to the Freaky Party" epitomises '80s synth programming, and **Jammin'** lives up to its title. The best ballad on the album, **My Dear Mr. Gaye**, is dedicated to Marvin Gaye, who, more than anyone, except Al Green, embodied the contradictions Marie is trying to unravel here: its pop idolatry indicates R&B's changing influences and goes some way to suggest why R&B's youngbloods don't have to wrestle with the same moral dilemmas.

⮌We almost chose **Greatest Hits**, Motown, 1985

49

Martha & the Vandellas

The Ultimate Collection

Motown, 1998

Although Martha & the Vandellas' records epitomised the Motown sound, Martha Reeves was probably the least typical Motown vocalist. The punchiest, sassiest, most assertive of all the label's female singers, her material may sometimes have been lame and lovelorn, but her gutsy voice meant it was impossible for her ever to sound demure.

Reeves had recorded a couple of solo records for the Checkmate label before joining Motown as an A&R secretary in the early 1960s. She eventually talked her way into singing on a demo and when the Andantes (Motown's troupe of female backing singers) couldn't make a studio date, Reeves and her bandmates from the Del-Phis, Annette Beard and Rosalind Ashford, replaced them. They were signed to Motown in 1962 and had their first hit in February 1963 with the rather banal **Come and Get These Memories**. A mere five months later the group and their producers/writers, Brian Holland, Lamont Dozier and Eddie Holland, would stamp their mark on pop music history.

With its heart-attack beat, honking baritone sax riff, dizzy piano chords and tumbling guitar intro, **(Love Is Like a) Heat Wave** had the same kind of relentless forward motion and visceral excitement that would make the Beatles the biggest thing since Fabian. As Beard and Ashford urged her on with "Go ahead girl" and "Don't pass up this chance", Reeves shouted and whooped and could barely be contained by the constraints of vinyl. As intense as its title suggested, "Heat Wave" scorched the long, hot summer as it screamed out of the speakers across the country. The formula was so good that the group's next two singles, **Quicksand** and **Live Wire**, were virtual note-for-note copies.

The Vandellas were starting to get into a rut, so they turned temporarily to Mickey Stevenson and Ivy Jo Hunter. The result was another definitive pop single, **Dancing in the Street**. Not only one of the great songs about getting down, "Dancing in the Street" derived much of its force from subtle references to the Civil Rights struggle. Lyrics like "This is an invitation across the nation, a chance for folks to meet", "Are you for a brand new beat?" and "Let's form a big strong line" seemed like wily double entendres, while that martial beat and whip-crack snare seemed to imitate the tramping of a million feet marching to the Capitol.

At the beginning of 1965 Beard was replaced by Betty Kelley and the Vandellas returned to the Holland-Dozier-Holland fold. Once again, the result was one of pop music's greatest moments, **Nowhere to Run**. Motown producer Norman Whitfield may have defined "paranoid soul" in the late '60s/early '70s, but the subgenre started here. Ashford and Kelley shadow Reeves' vocals like they're stalking her, while James Jamerson's bass-line and an insistent tambourine propel the music to almost unbearable levels of intensity. The flip-side was another song the group made with Stevenson and Hunter, and one of Motown's strangest. **Motoring** was a raunchy car metaphor straight out of the Robert Johnson songbook – in other words, the kind of song that Berry Gordy usually frowned upon. What made the record truly bizarre, though, was the weird backing track, which sounded slightly out of time, a result of Hunter running the tape backwards.

After "Nowhere to Run" Martha & the Vandellas would continue to have hits that were fine pop songs – like **My Baby Loves Me**, **I'm Ready for Love**, **Jimmy Mack** – but nothing anywhere near as epochal as their earlier masterpieces.

⟳We almost chose **Live Wire!**, Motown, 1993

50

Curtis Mayfield

Super Fly

Curtom, 1972

Like that other key falsetto voice of the 1960s, Smokey Robinson, Curtis Mayfield was more than just a very good soul singer. Just as Robinson was the main architect of the Motown sound, as a member of the Impressions, songwriter, producer, label owner and focal presence, Mayfield was the prime mover behind Chicago soul. Unlike Robinson, however, who remained a pop craftsman throughout his career (unless you count the wretched "Abraham, Martin and John" as social critique), Mayfield's music contains not only the gospel sound, but also gospel's sense of moral authority and uplift. He was one of the first soul artists to incorporate – with increasing explicitness – messages of black pride and self-determination into his music. Unlike James Brown, who couldn't have been any more strident on "Say It Loud – I'm Black and I'm Proud", Mayfield's messages were more gentle, built on the quiet righteousness of gospel rather than its more charismatic shrieks and hollers. Mayfield's music began to get tougher when he left the Impressions in 1970 to go solo, but while funk was getting ever more minimal, Mayfield's brand remained as detailed and as uplifting as his music of the '60s.

Mayfield's solo masterpiece is his soundtrack to the blaxploitation film, *Super Fly*. The film tells the story of a drug dealer named Priest who manages to leave the game with bags of money and escape from the ghetto with a good woman by his side. With its glamorisation of pushers and pimps, ridicule of community activists and message of "go out and get yours", the film has become one of the most influential cultural artefacts of the past thirty years. While Civil Rights activists Malcolm X and Black Panthers had tried to take the moral high ground, *Super Fly* presented a vision of the ghetto that was a dark, hopeless, mercenary inversion of the American Dream and people bought it by the bucketload.

Mayfield was one of the few who didn't. He saw that this glorification of the underworld was a dead end and conceived his soundtrack as a riposte to the film's message. However, when *Super Fly* showed in cinemas, it featured Mayfield's music but not his vocals. As such it's possible to criticise Mayfield's work for making Priest, and the rest of the film's rogues gallery, seem that much more heroic. Listen to the record, though, and his intentions become clear. Combined with Mayfield's lyrics, the Beatles-esque strings, the horns, flutes, detailed percussion, propulsive bass-lines and wah-wah guitar become a chorus of voices pleading for sanity.

The arrangements on **Super Fly** are incredible: what seems like talking drums chattering nervously on the intro to Pusherman are subsequently doubled by a choked wah-wah riff that suggests street trash being blown about by the wind; the funk symphony of Little Child Runnin' Wild; the sinister bass and guitar of Freddie's Dead undermined by the heavenly strings which are ultimately drowned out by an acerbic flute; the cheery piano and horns of No Thing On Me (Cocaine Song) which sound as unreal as the drug-fuelled fantasy that the song is about; the woodwinds challenging Superfly's pimp strut. With lyrics like "Let the man with the plan say he'd see him home/But his hope was a rope, and he should have known" and "The aim of his role was to move a lot of dough/Ask him his dream, what does it mean, he wouldn't know/Can't be like the rest is the most he'll confess/But the time is running out and there's no happiness", the music on *Super Fly* was perhaps the most challenging soul album of the entire era.

➲ We almost chose **Of All Time: Classic Collection**, Curtom, 1990

51

Harold Melvin & the Blue Notes

Wake Up Everybody

Remember, 1996

It wasn't just Kenny Gamble and Leon Huff's music – some of the greatest of the 1970s – that made their label, Philadelphia International, so remarkable; it was also the fact that that they achieved their best records with relatively obscure people. There again, the success of Gamble and Huff's rigid formula really depended on artists without ready-made images or personas. Their records with Wilson Pickett and Dusty Springfield, after all, weren't so hot. Whatever, just as they did with the journeymen harmony group, the O'Jays, Gamble and Huff turned a struggling Philadelphia vocal group called Harold Melvin & the Blue Notes into one of the premier R&B hit-machines of the decade.

Harold Melvin & the Blue Notes were formed in 1954 in the City of Brotherly Love as a doo-wop group. After winning the Amateur Night at the Apollo Theater in Harlem five weeks in succession, they recorded for small labels like Josie ("If You Love Me") and Value ("My Hero"). In the late '60s the group hired a local band called the Cadillacs (not the same group who did "Speedo" and "Gloria") to be their backing band on tour. In 1970, in mid-tour, the Blue Notes' lead singer, John Atkins, left the group and Melvin invited the Cadillacs' drummer to replace him. The drummer was Teddy Pendergrass and the career of one of the great male soul icons was born.

In 1971 the group reorganised around Pendergrass and signed to Philadelphia International, for whom their first release was "I Miss You". Creating what would become the group's basic formula, and the model for all subsequent soul singers, "I Miss You" features Pendergrass's gruff, baritone sermonising on the subject of love, backed by sweet harmonies from the Blue Notes. Although it was originally written for another former doo-wop group from Philadelphia, the Dells, "I Miss You" peaked at #6 on the R&B charts for Harold Melvin & the Blue Notes.

It was the follow-up, however, that was the group's calling card. Reaching the pop Top 3 and topping the R&B chart for two weeks, If You Don't Know Me By Now was one of the defining records of the '70s. Although "I Miss You" would presage the sound of black radio for the next two decades, it was too churchy for pop radio. "If You Don't Know Me By Now", however, streamlined and smoothed out the gospelese, adding a mass of strings to become the model for the crossover hits of the next few years. Irrespective of its historical significance, the song remains one of pop music's best evocations of a marriage breaking up – Pendergrass begs, pleads and harangues his wife, while the Blue Notes and the string section exude calm, patience and understanding.

The group's next big hit was 1973's The Love I Lost which, with its hissing hi-hats, driving beat, string obbligatos and histrionic vocals, became one of the building blocks of disco. 1975's Bad Luck, another dance-floor classic, has lines criticising the President and proves that disco wasn't just functional, robotic music. After an R&B #1 duet with Sharon Paige, Hope That We Can Be Together Soon, the Blue Notes recorded another potent disco message, Wake Up Everybody, which also went to the top of the R&B charts on the strength of its slow-building momentum and another rousing Pendergrass sermon. However, with Pendergrass leaving the Blue Notes to launch a solo career, it would be the group's last significant hit.

⤴We almost chose **The Best of Harold Melvin
& the Blue Notes**, Sony Legacy, 1995

The Meters

Funkify Your Life

Rhino, 1995

Though not as well trained as the mixed-race Creole bands, the black bands of New Orleans developed a style of playing that was "hotter" and more rhythmically charged than the Creoles' more European style. Meeting up on Sundays in the city's Congo Square, their musically competitive gatherings were known as "cutting sessions". The band who played the "hottest" would march in victory, accompanied by a "second line" of people following behind the band clapping, stomping and shouting along with the music. Rhythmically, this "second line" was a combination of John Philip Sousa with Latin American clavé patterns, and this syncopation is at the root of not only jazz, but just about every form of African-American music – especially funk.

The conversion of the marching-band style to the drum kit, was initiated by New Orleans beatsmith Earl Palmer – the father of funk. His example was followed by drummer Charles "Hungry", who took the marching-band gumbo flavour into more polyrhythmic directions. Hungry taught Clayton Fillyau, drummer on James Brown's *Live at the Apollo*, the New Orleans mandate and in his hands the James Brown beat was born.

For all of the Crescent City's rich funk tradition, however, its finest exponents were the Meters. Comprising organist Art Neville, bassist George Porter Jr., Guitarist Leo Nocentelli and drummer Joseph "Zigaboo" Modeliste, the Meters were effectively Allen Toussaint's house band from the mid-1960s onwards, where they played on records by Lee Dorsey and

Betty Harris. In 1969, the Meters started releasing their own instrumental material on the Josie label and immediately hit the R&B Top 10 with their version of a popular local dance, Sophisticated Cissy.

Probably the funkiest drummer to ever zing a Zildjian, Zigaboo Modeliste brought both the New Orleans tradition and the James Brown beat to hitherto unimagined levels of polyrhythmic dexterity. He may sound like an octopus behind the kit, but the reason he's such a bad-ass is that he keeps time like a Swiss quartz – it's not for nothing the band's called the Meters. But as their masterpiece, Look-Ka Py Py, shows, the Meters were not just about syncopation – no funk troupe had as strong a sense of the space between the beats. The holes were not just created by Zigaboo's outlandish grooves meeting Porter's bass precision, but by the unique comping of Neville and Nocentelli as well.

With Josie, the Meters would have ten R&B hits including Cissy Strut (another mind-boggling showcase for Ziggy's one-man second line), Chicken Strut (featuring the funkiest organ playing this side of Jimmy McGriff and a monumental bass breakdown) and Ease Back (which sounds like the Phantom of the Opera jamming with the canteen band from Star Wars). In 1972 the group signed with Reprise and added vocals courtesy of Neville to appease the major-label mind-set. Predictably, none of these recordings matched the quality of their instrumentals, but they still had plenty of gumbo flavour. Their best track from this period was the rare groove favourite, "Just Kissed My Baby".

Although **Funkify Your Life** doesn't feature any of their session work (their phenomenal grooves on Dr. John's *In the Right Place* album are well worth seeking out), it is the best available collection of their material. Divided into two discs, one covering their Josie period, the other the Reprise days, *Funkify Your Life* does an admirable job in sorting the wheat from the chaff and shows why they were voted World's Best Instrumental Group two years running.

⮑We almost chose **Look-Ka Py Py**, Rounder, 1990

53

Mulatu Astatqé

Éthiopiques 4: Ethio Jazz & Musique Instrumentale 1969–1974

Buda Musique, 1998

Soul music may have its roots firmly planted in the American South, but its pollen has scattered and fertilised all over the globe. There is no better proof of soul's universality than this mind-boggling collection of music from Ethiopian keyboard player Mulatu Astatqé.

The Éthiopiques series is a landmark excavation from the archives of Ethiopia's Amha Records, which was in operation between 1969 and 1978 before Mengistu's brutal dictatorship and the civil war brought Ethiopia's cultural scene to a halt. That this music survives at all is a miracle; that it's so good is a testament to music's life-affirming power. Quite simply, this is breathtaking stuff, with Astatqé's musicians revelling in the discovery and freedom of a new musical idiom. The impact, for jaded Western listeners, is exhilarating.

The instrumental music created by Mulatu Astatqé in the late '60s and early '70s is virtually unique in Ethiopia, since the culture of that country (like many of the countries surrounding the Red Sea) places a tremendous amount of emphasis on the word. Ethiopia largely avoided being colonised and so European instruments didn't take hold there until the country was briefly occupied by Mussolini in the late '30s. As one of the very few Ethiopian musicians to be educated abroad, Mulatu was familiar with jazz and the Beatles and thus realised that European instruments had rather more potential than the military marches and variations on "Finiculi Finicula" as learned from the Italians. Mulatu's Latin horn flourishes, conga rhythms, George Benson guitar riffs and Fender Rhodes licks further distanced his music from the mainstream of Ethiopia's 3000-year-old tradition. The end result of this synthesis is both familiar and slightly strange – jazz-funk played by highly skilled musicians suddenly finding themselves in a new and alien sound world teeming with new timbres and patterns.

There are few finer sounds than an outstanding musician newly discovering an effects pedal and there's plenty of outlandish soloing and riffing on **Éthiopiques 4**: the perfect wah-wah licks on **Yèkatit** and **Nètsanèt**, the flanger on **Gubèlyé**, the blissful fuzz guitar on **Yèkèrmo Sèw** and **Nètsanèt**, the Jimmy Smith/Mar-Keys organ transplant on **Yègellé Tezeta**. Elsewhere, there are echoes of Art Blakey & the Jazz Messengers, Isaac Hayes' score for *Truck Turner*, Duke Ellington and S.O.U.L. This jaw-dropping Afro-funk sounds like it was recorded in a high-school gym. But the crap fidelity and rawness of the recordings only adds to their charm and elevates Mulatu's arrangements above the unctuous realm inhabited by Roy Ayers and Lonnie Liston Smith, who both made their music out of similar materials. Some of this disc has appeared before on records put out by Crammed and Hannibal, and the music is so raw that it has found its way into the crates of certain hip-hop producers who shall remain nameless.

Of course, it's not simply the circumstances of the recording that makes the music so great. The album's final track, Dèwèl, was made in New York with Mongo Santamaria's band and could easily be the soundtrack to a blaxploitation flick. But Mulatu's take on '70s funk is more astringent, and thus harsher and more cutting, than his American contemporaries. It's hard to place quite where the difference lies, but there is something about Mulatu's ear and his timing that seem ever so slightly off-kilter when compared to the slickness of American funk, and it's in such sonic minutiae that Mulatu's true originality can be found.

⊃We almost chose **Various Artists – Éthiopiques 3**, Buda Musique, 1998

54

O'Jays

Back Stabbers

Philadelphia International, 1972

No one had more impact on music in the 1970s than producer-songwriters and Philadelphia International head honchos Kenny Gamble and Leon Huff. Perhaps the reason Philly International was so successful (at one point in the mid-'70s it was America's second most successful black-owned business after Motown) was that Gamble and Huff embodied the contradictions that threatened to tear black America apart in the early to mid-'70s: Kenny Gamble was a cultural nationalist whose music helped pave the way for the disco crossover; they preached about "cleaning up the ghetto", but aimed their records at the new hi-fi systems of the emerging African-American middle class; they wrote paternalistic message songs that often criticised masculinity. With gruff, assertive gospel leads contrasted against gossamer harmonies, the O'Jays' dialectic between the rough and smooth gave voice to the tensions at the heart of Gamble and Huff's vision and became the duo's greatest vehicle.

The O'Jays were a group of journeymen who had formed as a five-member vocal group in Canton, Ohio in 1958, calling themselves the Triumphs. Renaming themselves after a Cleveland disc jockey, Eddie O'Jay, in 1961, the group had a few minor hits for labels like Imperial and Bell throughout the '60s. By the time they became the first signings to Philadelphia International in 1972, the O'Jays were a trio of Eddie Levert, Walter Williams and William Powell, and by the time **Back Stabbers** came out they were no longer journeymen.

Back Stabbers begins with an almost mocking James Brown horn riff before modulating into a hard funk groove called **When the World's At Peace** that borrows heavily from Sly Stone. The first verse goes, "I can see the day when it's safe to walk the streets/When we'll learn to care for those lost in poverty/There'll be no need for our sons and daughters to march up and down the streets singing 'We Shall Overcome'", and its Civil Rights reference places this album in context.

Emerging from the percussion fog of "When the World's At Peace" is perhaps the greatest riff on the "smiling faces" trope of '70s soul, **Back Stabbers**. Recorded at a time when Nixon's Watergate treachery was just beginning to emerge, at a time when liberal senator Daniel Moynihan was blaming the cycle of poverty on African-American men, "Back Stabbers'" refrain of "Smilin' faces sometimes back stabbers" resonated with a significance that went far beyond the tale of a man whose friends want to steal his woman.

Who Am I is a brutally introspective track where Eddie Levert chastises himself for believing that men shouldn't cry and for not listening to her enough. On the second side, however, "Back Stabbers" is remade as the punchier **992 Arguments**, in which Levert rails, "I'm supposed to be the one wearing the pants around here", to a background of keyboards losing their composure, furious guitars, surging waves of strings and a bassline that just snaps. Elsewhere, Levert is plagued by **Shiftless, Shady, Jealous Kind of People**, but in amongst all the trouble and strife are the stolen moments of bliss of **Listen to the Clock on the Wall**, which are inevitably tempered because they both have to go home to their spouses.

The final track, **Love Train**, introduced some levity to the album and became the O'Jays' only pop #1. You'd almost expect the lyrics to be from some wispy flower child like Scott McKenzie, but the O'Jays give it some old-time religion and turn "Love Train" into secular gospel of the highest order.

> ↰We almost chose **The Philly Sound: Kenny Gamble, Leon Huff and the Story of Brotherly Love 1966–1976**, Sony, 1997

55

Parliament

Funkentelechy vs. the Placebo Syndrome

Casablanca, 1977

Perhaps George Clinton's greatest funk opera, **Funkentelechy vs. the Placebo Syndrome** ensured that Uncle Jam would go down in the history books as pop music's most inspired lunatic. Listening back to this absurdist *tour de force*, it's mind-boggling that this Ionesco-esque sci-fi fantasy actually sold a million copies. Maybe drugs really were stronger back then! Yet, in fairness to its creator, Clinton's supreme gift (not unlike his idol Sly Stone) lay in his ability to combine a piercing intelligence with populist grooves, thus creating the most potent kind of pop music.

Funkentelechy was the refinement of Clinton's slyly facetious futurism following the success of the mammoth P-Funk Earth Tour, which had a (then unheard of) $275,000 budget for descending Motherships, space pimp outfits and toy bop guns. For *Funkentelechy*, Clinton and gang turned the Earth Tour's visual spectacle into an aural Las Vegas of grotesque overload, *Satyricon*-like perversity, total sensual gratification, dancing girls, bright lights, Marvel comics brought to life, naughty fairy-tales and gratuitous special effects. The star of the show, and the man who brought Clinton's crazed inventions to life, was Bernie Worrell, whose synth fugues and keyboard squiggles were the sonic equivalent of one of Yves Tanguy's surrealist landscapes, yet somehow perfectly in sync with the blues continuum.

Mothership Connection's protagonist, Star Child, returned for this tale of cloning and mind control as "the protector of the pleasure principle" who invades the "zone of zero funkativity" in order to make the villain, Sir Nose D'Voidoffunk, dance and thus defeat the "Placebo Syndrome" with his "Bop Gun". **Funkentelechy** weaved an attack on advertising and commodity fetishism into this cartoon parable by introducing the notion that capitalism's "urge overkill' was "pimping the funk". "Funkentelechy"'s narrators have to rescue "the pleasure principle" from Sir Nose's snake-oil salesmen who control your mind with ad slogans and catch phrases. For all the power of "the pleasure principle" and the jokes about McDonald's and Anacin, Clinton doesn't let you forget what really matters: "Funking is easier than paying attention."

Clinton's comic-book scenarios always obscured his messages behind the cartoon music and juvenile humour, but it was hard to ignore **Bop Gun**'s reference to the Civil Rights struggle: "Turn me loose, we shall overcome."

The "Bop Gun" was Clinton's metaphor for the life-affirming power of dancing in the face of the pleasure-denying, sexless Puritans who still ran America 200 years after they founded it. With the album's closing track, **Flash Light**, Clinton found a song that made his metaphor real: only a completely joyless fucker with a rump of steel skin could possibly deny it.

"Flash Light" was not only a landmark for its implausibly kinetic groove, but for its groundbreaking use of technology as well. By taking advantage of the Moog's capacity for stacking notes on top of each other to create a gargantuan bass sound, Worrell's synth bass-line on "Flash Light" remains perhaps the most important musical moment of the past 25 years as it anticipated and allowed the use of synths as rhythm machines. Released in the same year as Kraftwerk's *Trans-Europe Express* and Donna Summer's "I Feel Love", "Flash Light" helped make the world safe for the electronic revolution and proved that synthesizers didn't originate in the "zone of zero funkativity" and didn't necessarily ring the death knell for humanity.

⤺We almost chose **Motorbooty Affair**, Casablanca, 1978

56

Parliament

Mothership Connection

Casablanca, 1975

Most commentators have noted that Parliament aimed for the butt, while Funkadelic aimed for the mind. The irony, of course, is that this was precisely the kind of Cartesian, racist dualism that George Clinton was attempting to deconstruct in the first place. The truth is that Funkadelic, Clinton's guitar band, was playing "white" rock music while concerning itself with the groupie fantasies and adult fairy-tales from a Rudy Ray Moore or Redd Foxx album. Parliament, Clinton's groove band, was playing the funkiest music in creation while creating grandiose albums that mocked the Beatles or Pink Floyd in their conceptual complexity. Daring you to make assumptions about his music, Clinton was the industry's greatest trickster and, as he was fond of saying, he was often "gamin' on ya".

1975's **Mothership Connection** was the first in Parliament's series of "funk operas". Coming out of the same jam sessions that produced the basic tracks for Funkadelic's *Let's Take it to the Stage* and Bootsy Collins' *Stretchin' Out in Bootsy's Rubber Band*, *Mothership Connection* would prove to be Parliament-Funkadelic's commercial breakthrough with **Give Up the Funk (Tear the Roof Off the Sucker)** reaching the American Top 15 on the strength of a preposterously funky groove and catch phrase. Like the great synthesist that he is, Clinton took the Afro-futurist musical ideas that were circulating at the time on albums by Miles Davis, Herbie Hancock and Sun Ra, boiled them down into a form digestible by the pop audience and placed them in a comic-book world rich in both humour and metaphor.

For those with proofreader's eyes, *Mothership Connection*'s blend of outer-space myth and Methodist mumbo jumbo was highlighted on the sleeve credits ("Extraterrestrial Voices & Good Time Hand Clappers"); everyone else would have to wait for the music. The DJ from the previous *Chocolate City* album was resurrected in the persona of Star Child, who "returned to claim the Pyramids" in the Mothership from the "chocolate Milky Way". Gospel's deliverance was no longer brought forth by the white cherubs of European imagination, but by chitlin'-eating, Afro-clad brothers from another planet. The "sweet chariot" of slave-era spirituals became a spaceship offering escape from the ghetto via **Supergroovalisticprosifunkstication**. In Clinton's future, funk replaced religion and became the object of trans-galactic crusades by **Unfunky UFOs**. **Handcuffs**, the one track that seemed out of place in this tech-gnostic revelation of the infinite, just happened to be Clinton's most harrowing and bizarre expression of lover's paranoia, even if it was played for laughs.

The depth of Clinton's sci-fi fantasy was matched by the creation of a unique sound world. Bootsy's custom-made Space Bass and Bigfoot Brailey's well-named drums laid down an unfeasibly aqueous, molten bottom over which guitarists Michael Hampton and Garry Shider vamped in tiny gestures and with rocket-science precision. Bernie Worrell's trademark high-pitched synth squiggles really started taking shape on *Mothership Connection* as he sculpted the contours of Clinton's outer-space in sound.

None of this would have translated outside of Clinton's twisted consciousness were it not for compositions that took funk's gift for the catch phrase and crafted it into full-blown songs. **P. Funk (Wants to Get Funked Up)** was a hypnotic, spaced-out groove mantra, while **Mothership Connection (Star Child)** was a collage of hepcat phrases, street jive and old spirituals that Clinton wove into a coherent, but demented, cartoon parable. Meanwhile, "Unfunky UFO" and **Night of the Thumpasorus Peoples** were like George Romero flicks with high production values come to life. In other words, *Mothership Connection* was funk's Book of Revelation.

⊃We almost chose **The Best of Parliament: Give Up the Funk**, Mercury, 1995

57

Ann Peebles

How Strong Is a Woman – The Story of Ann Peebles (1969–80)

Cream/Hi Records, 1998

Memphis' Hi Records will be forever associated with Al Green, but during the same period St Louis-born soulstress Ann Peebles created a body of work that is equally distinctive and almost as definitive as that of her more famous labelmate. While Green was redefining the soulman as a softly spoken gentleman capable of commitment, Peebles injected the long-suffering female soul persona with rage and rootsiness. Unlike the somewhat gimmicky feminism of Laura Lee, Peebles sang from a strong woman's perspective without abandoning the gospel-blues tradition. This excellent two-CD compilation of her time at Hi surveys all her albums with the label and is the only Peebles collection anyone needs to own.

Peebles' first single was 1969's **Walk Away**. One of Hi main-man Willie Mitchell's first productions, "Walk Away" was a classic Memphis blend of gospel feeling and country chords. While Peebles' phrasing was reminiscent of Aretha Franklin's, her voice was more direct, more ragged, more love-worn – scarcely the sound of a 22-year-old. Unfortunately, with slightly awkward covers of hits like Bettye Swann's **Make Me Yours**, her debut album, *This Is Ann Peebles*, never managed to live up to the power of "Walk Away".

In 1970, however, her version of the blues evergreen, **Part Time Love**, and her album of the same name, truly established Peebles as a great, if underappreciated, singer. Although "Part

Time Love" had been a standard for male singers, it was tailor-made for Peebles' tough, assertive wail and she attacked it with real relish. The other outstanding tracks from this album which feature on **How Strong Is a Woman**, are Peebles' self-penned I'll Get Along – a bluesy, testifying declaration of independence – and the devastating slow-burn, I Still Love You.

Her 1972 cover version of Bobby Bland's I Pity the Fool followed the same blueprint as "Part Time Love" to become another profound blast of break-up catharsis. "I Pity the Fool" was one of two highlights on her *Straight From the Heart* album. The other was her definitive reading of I Feel Like Breaking Up Somebody's Home. Once again, Peebles brought her forceful pipes and a feminine perspective to bear on a classic male cheating song, and the results rank alongside Aretha's reading of Otis Redding's "Respect".

Despite their perfect Southern soul credentials, Peebles' albums failed to sell and it wasn't until 1973 that she made the commercial breakthrough with I Can't Stand the Rain. Its instantly memorable beginning sounds more like it emerged from a Parisian sound lab than Willie Mitchell's Memphis studios, but with Al Jackson's smouldering drums, a driving piano and, above all, Peebles' ravaged vocals, "I Can't Stand the Rain" remains one of the true classics of the Memphis sound. Although it only reached #38, it was still Peebles' biggest pop hit and something of a minor miracle that so naked and raw a song could make the charts at all.

While "I Can't Stand the Rain" was Peebles' own property (co-written with husband Don Bryant), only fools and Paul Young would dare to challenge her classic cover version of I'm Gonna Tear Your Playhouse Down. Although Willie Mitchell's by now formulaic production was perfectly suited for Al Green, it didn't always work with Peebles, and this is definitely one record where she outperformed her band and saved the record.

While the mid to late '70s recordings collected here are a series of diminishing returns – with the backing becoming increasingly faceless – Peebles remains a great singer always capable of transcending tired musicians and weak material.

⮑We almost chose **Straight From the Heart**, Hi, 1972

58

Wilson Pickett

Wilson Pickett's Greatest Hits

Atlantic, 1987

Journalist Dave Marsh has said that if Wilson Pickett "came along today, he'd be a rapper". It's hard to disagree with him – no one this side of Ice Cube has more 'tude than "the Wicked Pickett". While it's true that no matter how far away from the speakers you sit Pickett always sounds like he's in your face – his voice so ravaged it's as if he'd just downed more bottles of St. Ides than an entire cipher of Compton rappers – Pickett hits you with an emotional, gospel-derived force that no MC could hope to attain.

Born in Alabama in 1941, Pickett first came to prominence in Detroit as a member of the legendary Falcons. During their career the Falcons featured Eddie Floyd, Sir Mack Rice, and Joe Stubbs (who later found success as part of 100 Proof Aged in Soul) as well as Pickett. Their 1959 single, "You're So Fine", is often cited as "the first soul record", but it was their 1962 smash, I Found a Love, which was their best record. With backing supplied by the Ohio Untouchables (who would soon become the Ohio Players), "I Found a Love" featured Pickett's amazingly powerful tenor lead. Pickett went solo after and suffered the injustice of having Atlantic release a version of his "If You Need Me" by Solomon Burke that effectively destroyed the chart potential of his record.

Nonetheless, in 1964 Pickett was signed by Atlantic. He struggled for the next year with unsuitable material and was almost dropped from the label until he went to Memphis to record at the Stax studio. The first song that Pickett and guitarist Steve Cropper came up with was **In the Midnight Hour**, which became Pickett's first hit and established him as one of the titans of '60s soul. With a definitive Memphis horn line and drums inspired by producer Jerry Wexler's attempt to do The Jerk, "In the Midnight Hour" was the perfect background for Pickett's throat-shredding vocals. Based on Dorothy Love Coates' 1956 gospel classic "99 ½", Pickett's next single was one of the definitive soul singles. For those in the know, **Ninety-Nine and a Half Won't Do** was a blasphemous transmogrification of religious ecstasy into the most salacious lust – dig the way he licks his chops as he says, "Ain't no use in foolin' ourselves honey", as the song fades out.

"Ninety-Nine and a Half Won't Do" was pure evil transposed to vinyl and failed to make much of an impression on the charts, but his next single was all sweetness and light and stayed atop the R&B charts for seven weeks. **634-5789 (Soulsville, U.S.A.)** was a bit singsong-y, but it proved that Pickett could do more than rupture his diaphragm and revealed an emotional range equal to anyone. His next R&B chart-topper, a cover of Chris Kenner's **Land of 1,000 Dances**, was based largely on Cannibal & the Headhunters' garage-punk version. The record is a bundle of compressed energy, with the horns breaking up on impact and Roger Hawkins' pile-driving drums pushing Pickett to rip his larynx asunder on the final "Ahh, help me"s. Although it couldn't match the grit of the original, Pickett's version of Dyke & the Blazers' **Funky Broadway** continued his reign as the king of the dance floor and was once again an R&B #1.

Mustang Sally returned Pickett to the wicked terrain that he had made his own with "Ninety-Nine and a Half Won't Do" and became one of his most well-known records. If you only know the Commitments' version, do yourself a favour and get this pronto.

⮌ We almost chose **A Man and a Half**, Rhino, 1992

59

Prince

Dirty Mind

Warner Bros., 1980

Somebody at Warner Brothers must have been in touch with the spirits when an 18-year-old nobody from nowhere (Minneapolis, Minnesota, to be precise) and his manager and attorney managed to negotiate a deal that allowed the artist to produce himself. Almost unprecedented in the history of major labels, particularly for a black artist (only Stevie Wonder had been granted such complete artistic control so young), the relative creative control given to Prince allowed "His Royal Badness" to explore his personal vision to the full and it finally came to fruition on his third and most sexually explicit album to date, **Dirty Mind**.

Not since James Brown's *Sex Machine* had an album's title so matched its contents. After running away from home at the age of 14, Prince Rogers Nelson eventually ended up living in the basement of his friend's mother's house. It was here that he began writing songs, cutting himself off from the outside world and jotting down his fantasies in a notebook. With stories that could have been straight from the letter pages of *Penthouse* and produced, arranged, written and recorded almost completely by Prince, *Dirty Mind* begat the narcissism that plagues the contemporary R&B scene. While subsequent singers followed his lead on subject matter, none of them have been able to duplicate his vocal skill. The best falsetto singer of the last thirty years, Prince's vocal chops prevent his salacious tales from descending into mere vanity.

Dirty Mind's sleeve art, which looks a lot like covers of records by the Jam and the Knack, should give you a clue as to the music inside. *Dirty Mind* is Prince's most new wave album: the guitars are all trebly, the synth riffs are simple and direct and some of the harmonies just scream skinny-tie band. Because of this, the material may have dated a bit in a way that *1999* (aside from its title) or *Purple Rain,* with their supreme pop craftsmanship, won't. That said, *Dirty Mind* does contain **When You Were Mine**, a pop song that could have been as transcendent and enduring as "1999" or "Little Red Corvette" or "I Wanna Be Your Lover" or "When Doves Cry", and *Dirty Mind* remains one of Prince's biggest aesthetic triumphs. "When You Were Mine" comes out of the speakers like something by alterna-traditionalists the Silos, but the lyrics are anything but weedy indie-pop – "You didn't have the decency to change the sheets", "I was never the kind to make a fuss/When you were there sleeping in between the two of us" – making it one of the best songs ever about a *ménage à trois.*

Elsewhere, on top of sharp synth melodies and deep funk grooves that were among the best of the era, the lyrical details are a little less radio-friendly. Propelled by a bass-line that could have been found on a Depeche Mode or Yazoo record, **Dirty Mind** was all filth and perdition: "In my Daddy's car, it's you I really want to drive". **Uptown**, where he sleeps with a stranger that picked him up on the street during an orgy, is his idea of utopia. This is nothing, however, compared to what are, inevitably, the best tracks on the album. On **Head**, the most straightforwardly funky cut on *Dirty Mind*, sees the singer bird-dog a bride on the way to her wedding and then climax on her wedding dress. Over another amped-up new wave guitar track, Prince sings about the joys of incest on **Sister**. Then, on **Partyup**, he tries to justify everything by writing an anti-war song, claiming it was "revolutionary rock'n'roll".

⊃We almost chose **1999**, Warner Bros., 1982

Prince

Sign o' the Times

Paisley Park, 1987

Prince was the pop star *par excellence* of the 1980s for two reasons. In a time of faceless, corporate soul by the likes of Luther Vandross and Freddie Jackson, Prince was probably the only R&B artist able to synthesise his influences into an original vision. Perhaps more importantly, Prince was the only black performer, aside from a handful of hip-hop artists, to address the hopelessness and spiritual desolation of the Reagan years. Like a century of African-American musicians before him, this was often channelled into bitter love songs and a ribaldry so fierce that it would make Chaucer or Petronius blush. As its use of the peace sign in its title indicated (not to mention the sound of his music), however, Prince was also infatuated with the often politically explicit, psychedelic soul of the late '60s/early '70s, and **Sign o' the Times** unites these two facets like no album since Marvin Gaye's *What's Going On* and Sly & the Family Stone's *There's a Riot Goin' On*.

Prince produced and recorded *Sign o' the Times* pretty much on his own. Despite (or perhaps because of) this solipsism, *Sign o' the Times* is Prince's most referential album. With his super-high falsetto, the occasionally mumbling vocals and the funk scribbles, Sign o' the Times sounded a lot like Marvin Gaye's "You're the Man" and "Trouble Man". The drum machine on the title track referenced Sly Stone's "There's a Riot Goin' On", even as it retained a hope and faith in love and sex that Sly couldn't muster. U Got the Look was what the James Brown guitar riff would sound like if the star of his band was Eddie Van Halen and not Bootsy Collins. **It's Gonna Be a Beautiful Night** and **Housequake** were both P-Funk redux. **If I Was Your Girlfriend** could have been an ode to Sylvester, the only falsetto vocalist who out-gender-fucks Prince. **The Cross** was an outrageous combination of gospel and the Velvet Underground, or at least *New York*-era Lou Reed.

Sign o' the Times doesn't rely on history to make its point, however. Like *There's a Riot Goin' On*, the songs were often so muted that they felt half-finished. Unlike *There's a Riot Goin' On*, though, *Sign o' the Times* wasn't in any way sapped of energy. Tracks like "If I Was Your Girlfriend", "The Cross" and "Sign o' the Times" were abstract, to be sure, but Prince's vocal chops filled them out and pushed them over the top into the realm of pure pop. Then there were the grooves. "It's Gonna Be a Beautiful Night" was recorded live in Paris with the Revolution and absolutely smokes. "U Got the Look" was slamming, but it was also something far more than an intense funk track. The album's title track contextualised the record by mentioning AIDS (that "big disease with a little name") in the very first line.

With the Parents Music Resource Center already on Prince's back for writing songs about masturbation and incest, he came up with the most dangerous record of his career. It may very well feature the vacant dance-pop chanteuse Sheena Easton (another object of PMRC scorn) and a passage bordering on Meatloaf's "Paradise By the Dashboard Light", but by combining seething funk with heavy-metal guitar and with lines like "Your body's heck-a-slammin'/If love is good, let's get to rammin'", "U Got the Look" was a melting pot of the moral guardians' two most hated forms of music that was all about quick, intense sex without thinking about the consequences. If Prince's obsession with freaky sex often sounded merely like a shock tactic, this was where it coalesced into something more than an erotic fantasy.

◗We almost chose **Purple Rain**, Warner Bros., 1984

61

Otis Redding

Dreams to Remember: The Otis Redding Anthology

Atlantic, 1998

Otis Redding's best records seem so timeless, so full of hard-earned authority that it's hard to believe that he was only 26 when he died in a plane crash in 1967. The very embodiment of the "soulman", Redding was all grits, grunt and gospel fire. But rather than becoming little more than a caricature, Redding used his overwhelming presence to tap into the recesses of emotion that most men find so hard to express. His stylistic excess wasn't grotesque melodrama, but the sound of someone so sensitive that his feelings only came out in floods.

Born in 1941 in Dawson, Georgia, Redding grew up dirt poor in nearby Macon. He dropped out of high school early to front Little Richard's old band, the Upsetters. Redding's formative influences represented the twin poles of soul style – the shriek of Little Richard and the grace of Sam Cooke – but his first records were largely imitative of the former. Redding's second record, Shout Bamalama (recorded in 1960 with Macon group the Pinetoppers, and included here), was pure Little Richard, but by the time of his first record at the Stax studio, Redding's fusion of the two was complete. These Arms of Mine was an impromptu recording made after Redding had floored Stax head Jim Stewart and after most of the musicians had finished for the day. With guitarist Steve Cropper sitting in for keyboardist Booker T. Jones, the arrangement was as basic as anything you'd hear at a 10-year-old's piano recital, but it laid out what would become the blueprint for country soul.

1963's **Pain in My Heart** continued in similar fashion by ripping off New Orleans producer Allen Toussaint and vocalist Irma Thomas's "Ruler of My Heart". Redding's version was just as good and took the song to its rightful place in the pop charts. The formula was perfected, however, on 1965's **I've Been Loving You Too Long (To Stop Now)**. Written by Redding with Chicago soulman Jerry Butler, "I've Been Loving You Too Long" was tailor-made for Redding's style: lovemen will forever try to copy it, but only Redding could get away with those quavering notes and the pleading outro without turning it into an orgy of mawkishness.

Just as good, but never released as a single, was his reading of Eddie Thomas, Jerry Butler and Roy Lowe's **Cigarettes and Coffee** from 1966. From the bleary horns to Booker T.'s ghost-town saloon keyboard to Al Jackson's exhausted beat, the arrangement of "Cigarettes and Coffee" evokes its quarter-to-three-in-the-morning atmosphere perfectly. Then, Redding comes in singing this smouldering ballad as if it was his last shot at keeping the relationship together. Most amazing of all might have been his reading of **Try a Little Tenderness**, an old piece of Tin Pan Alley frippery that in Redding's hands became a desperate plea.

Of course, Redding was equally adept at uptempo songs. **Fa-Fa-Fa-Fa-Fa (Sad Song)** might have been little more than a few lines about soul music attached to some nonsense syllables, but Redding sings it like it contains the meaning of life. Riding one of the greatest drumbeats ever, **Tramp** has Redding playing a hayseed defending himself against the vicious taunts of cosmopolitan Carla Thomas to create the most irresistible of all the battle-of-the-sexes records. Amazingly, the only time Redding ever reached the pop Top 20 was with the last song he recorded before he died, the meditative, weary, semi-acoustic and eternal **(Sittin' On) The Dock of the Bay**.

⮑We almost chose **The Very Best of Otis Redding**, Rhino, 1993

62

Smokey Robinson & the Miracles

The Tracks of My Tears

Spectrum, 1997

Smokey Robinson was famously called "America's greatest living poet" by no less an authority than Bob Dylan. Robinson wasn't necessarily one of popular music's great songwriters because of his words, however. His lyrics were often rather trite, but his command of meter, rhyme and turn of phrase elevated his songs above the realm of pop schmaltz and into the rarefied air of, well, poetry. While no one had done as much for vernacular language since Gutenberg, Robinson's biggest artistic triumph might have been his image. He wasn't a great singer, but his wounded, fragile, doo-wop-influenced high tenor admitted a vulnerability that few, if any, black male singers before him had dared, and his vision of love rather than lust paved the way for such non-traditional male personas as Al Green, the Stylistics and the Delfonics.

Robinson formed the Miracles in 1957 with Ron White, Warren "Pete" Moore, Bobby Rogers and Claudette Rogers. They auditioned for, and failed to impress, Jackie Wilson's manager, but there they met Berry Gordy Jr., who was impressed with their voices and with Robinson's catalogue of 100 songs. The group's first release, "Got a Job", an answer song to the Silhouettes' "Get a Job", hit the R&B charts, but it wasn't until 1960's **Shop Around**, though, that the group would establish themselves – and Motown (it was the label's first million-seller) – as a permanent fixture on the pop charts. 1962's "I'll Try Something New" surrounded Robinson in echo and strings, marking it as the first Motown record to go for the pop charts with unrestrained ambition.

With its opening line, "I don't like you, but I love you", 1963's You've Really Got a Hold on Me truly established Robinson as the poet laureate of the lovelorn. Ooo Baby Baby embodied Robinson's art: the rhythm of his lyrics blend with his impossibly high, lachrymose vocals, set in an arrangement that would be imitated hundreds of times, to create a record more moving than the lyrics would convey (check Linda Ronstadt's for proof). Robinson's masterpiece, however, was probably The Tracks of My Tears. Again, lines like "My smile is my make-up I wear since my break-up with you" come to life inside an arrangement that welds classic crooning and street-corner harmony to one of the great Motown beats that studio band the Funk Brothers would come up with.

Of course, Robinson also wrote great dance music. "I Gotta Dance to Keep From Crying", "Come On Do the Jerk", Mickey's Monkey and Going to a Go-Go were all proof of his multifaceted talent. Like all great craftsmen, he was never content with leaving them as mere dance craze trifles, and all of them had moments of pure Smokey poetry. Catapulted by one of James Jamerson's defining bass-lines and perfect percussion, I Second That Emotion blended both a dance imperative and heartbreak like few others. With lyrics like "Maybe you want to give me kisses sweet/But only for one night with no repeat", "I Second That Emotion" sounded more like a Shirelles song than something by a male soul singer, and its portrait of male vulnerability has yet to be topped.

After Robinson left the Miracles in 1972, he used his voice for very different ends. With his 1975 album, *A Quiet Storm*, he single-handedly created the "quiet storm" subgenre of late-night, adult-oriented ballads that emphasised whispered vocals and ornate orchestrations, proving once again that he was one of popular music's singular talents.

⊃We almost chose **A Quiet Storm**, Motown, 1975

63

Sam & Dave

The Best of Sam & Dave

Atlantic, 1987

For four years and ten singles, the greatest duo in the history of pop music languished on fairly obscure Miami soul labels. While Sam Moore and Dave Prater were saddled with lame material, much of the blame must be laid at their own feet. By trying to be a pair of Sam Cookes, Sam & Dave just sounded like everybody else at the time. The turning point came in 1965, when they were signed by Atlantic, who packed them off to the Stax studios in Memphis. Over the next few years, working primarily with the songwriting/production team of Isaac Hayes and David Porter, Sam & Dave made some of the hardest and deepest soul records ever to cross into the mainstream.

Released in March 1965, Sam & Dave's first record at Stax was David Porter's solo composition, Goodnight Baby. With Prater singing lead, "Goodnight Baby" wasn't typical of the duo's output, but the gospel testifying at the end introduced what would become their signature. Their second Stax effort, I Take What I Want, written by Porter and Hayes, was a stomping tale of sexual urgency, this time featuring Moore's straining lead. Like that other great rasper, James Brown, Moore wanted to be smooth and slick, but Hayes and Porter encouraged him to sing above his natural register, making the vocals that much more intense and anxious.

By the time of 1966's You Don't Know Like I Know, the formula was just about perfected. Based on the gospel standard, "You Don't Know What the Lord Has Done For Me", the track has Sam & Dave alternating preaching ad-libs over a popping arrangement that slowly builds until it crashes on top of you. If "You Don't Know Like I Know" was just barely kept from boiling over, their next single, **Hold On, I'm Comin'**, was such a cauldron of energy that you could practically feel the sweat pouring from the speakers. One of the funkiest records ever, "Hold On" features a mean chicken-scratch riff from guitarist Steve Cropper, and drummer Al Jackson Jr. doing his version of June Gardner's bad-ass "Get Out of My Life Woman" beat. On top of the instrumental ferment, Sam & Dave traded lines like they were running away from the flames.

"Hold On, I'm Comin'", which topped the R&B chart and reached #21 in the pop charts, spawned several other brimstone-and-fire sermons of lust. **You Got Me Hummin'** followed, with slow-burn riffing, classic Memphis horns and a whole lot of "unnngghh". 1967's **Soul Man** was the bragging-est song this side of Bo Diddley, with a searing guitar lick that was every bit as elemental as Diddley's; 1968's **I Thank You** found the duo singing hosannas about being baptised in love (while preparing the world for Hayes' penchant for the clavinet). At the time, Sam & Dave and Hayes and Porter were so hot that even "I Thank You"'s flip side, "Wrap it Up", was a smoking girl-watching classic.

Although they were responsible for some of the most sexually predatory records ever made, Sam & Dave were just as effective on the tender, slow numbers. Their harmonies were tailor-made for the Mahalia-style arrangements and they got both river deep and mountain high on one of the truly great soul ballads, **When Something Is Wrong With My Baby**. By 1967, Sam & Dave had proved their worth and were allowed to indulge their Sam Cooke fantasies by recording the great man's **Soothe Me**. While they retained Cooke's sense of phrasing, Sam & Dave were no longer slavish imitators. Instead, they had become two of soul music's greatest and most individual stylists.

⮑We almost chose **The Very Best of Sam & Dave**, Rhino, 1995

64

The Shirelles

The Very Best of the Shirelles

Rhino, 1994

One of the standard articles of rock'n'roll faith is that there was no good music made between Buddy Holly's death and the arrival of the Beatles. The reason for this bit of dogma is clear: this was the era of the girl group and, as all serious music fans know, teenage girls are responsible for the worst music. Of course, this is preposterous – the same kind of racist (not to mention sexist) nonsense that holds that jazz wasn't radical until Charlie Parker came along. The fact that girl groups, particularly the Shirelles, provided much of the material for the British Invasion usually goes unmentioned: the Beatles, Manfred Mann and the Merseybeats all covered Shirelles songs. Two articles of faith that you *can* believe in, however, are that the Shirelles were among the first of the girl groups – the first after the Chantels to have any real success – and they were the best.

Originally called the Poquellos, the Shirelles (Shirley Owens, Beverly Lee, Doris Kenner and Addie "Micki" Harris) were "discovered" by their schoolmate Mary Jane Greenberg at a school dance in Passaic, New Jersey. Greenberg's mother, Florence, owned a small record label and in 1959 she formed the Scepter label as an outlet for girls. At the time, the majority of the vocal groups were male, but the virginal playground chanting of 1958's **I Met Him on a Sunday (Ronde-Ronde)** and the panting melodrama of 1960's **Tonight's the Night** would soon change all that.

The big breakthrough, though, was 1960's **Will You Still Love Me Tomorrow**. Working with producer Luther Dixon, a former R&B singer who had written and produced songs for Perry Como, the Shirelles crafted probably the most enduring record about female sexuality ever made. Of course, Gerry Goffin and Carole King's lyrics and melody made that task pretty easy, but the zing-went-the-strings-of-my-heart production and surging beat which were borrowed from the Drifters, not to mention Shirley Owens' heartbreakingly naive vocals, are what really made the record.

Perhaps even better was their rendition of **Dedicated to the One I Love**. Originally released in 1959, "Dedicated" would eventually climb to #3 in the pop charts in 1961. With its plaintive lead vocal and thrilling doo-wop swoops, "Dedicated" took the puppy love romantic ideals of doo-wop away from the pretty-boy singers and put them in the mouths of the teenage girls who actually bought the records.

The Shirelles weren't all sweetness and light, however. **Mama Said** has a chorus with more schoolgirl sass than just about any other girl group record; **Big John** has the kind of rollicking blues rhythm more associated with macho nogood-niks; while **Baby It's You**, with its outrageous organ solo, "cheat, cheat" chorus and Owens' brilliant vocals, says just about everything you need to know about why nice girls fall in love with bad boys. Produced by the inventor of The Hustle, Van McCoy, **Stop the Music** is the best cat fight this side of Crystal and Alexis trading blows on *Dynasty*, while **Foolish Little Girl** dishes up some painful truths. **Boys**, which would be covered by the Beatles on their first album, was all simmering lust and its arrangement would soon come to signify the swinging '60s.

After the #1 success of Soldier Boy and the Top 10 position of "Foolish Little Girl", the hits dried up. However, it wasn't only the British Invasion that stalled the Shirelles' career: the success of their labelmate and unofficial "fifth Shirelle" Dionne Warwick meant that they were soon forced to take the back seat.

↪We almost chose **The Best of the Crystals**, ABKCO, 1992

65

Percy Sledge

It Tears Me Up: The Best of Percy Sledge

Atlantic, 1992

Percy Sledge, or more precisely songwriters Cameron Lewis and Andrew Wright, wasn't the first (and he certainly won't be the last) artist to have a song completely misunderstood by the majority of his audience. Sledge's most famous record is, of course, When a Man Loves a Woman – a record that was not only the first Southern soul record to hit #1 in the US pop charts (in 1966), but probably the most-played slow-dance record of all time. You've probably heard it a thousand times, but if you actually listen to it carefully it's not quite what it seems. Although couples embrace tightly and shuffle slowly across dance floors around the world to "When a Man Loves a Woman", it (or at least the lyrics) don't exactly make you want to cuddle up to your loved one.

A mixture of a cautionary tale about being played for a fool and a plea to a woman not to take advantage of the singer, "When a Man Loves a Woman" is a forlorn ballad in the classic Southern soul tradition. While the funereal organ and the ticktocking cymbal work seem to indicate that the singer and his "loving eyes that don't see" are going to repeat the same mistakes all over again, Sledge doesn't quite sing it that way. It's the strange compassion and understanding that he brings to the song that makes it such an enduring standard. Singing like he's resigned to the fact that he's doomed to love the wrong woman, but determined that his passion won't be taken for granted this time, Sledge turns the song into an affirmation of the power of love to transcend all reason.

It's this combination of passion and long-sufferance that makes Percy Sledge one of the finest Southern soul singers. An unholy conjugation of Ernest Tubb and Otis Redding, Sledge combined the boohoos of country with the pow of soul. Born in Leighton, Alabama, in 1941, Sledge made his best records in nearby Sheffield – under the auspices of local disc jockey Quin Ivy – with the same session men who would make the name of Fame Studios in nearby Muscle Shoals: guitarist Jimmy Johnson, organist Spooner Oldham, bassist Junior Lowe and drummer Roger Hawkins. It's not just that all these guys – aside from Sledge – were white that make his music (and Southern soul in general) remarkable, it was the fact that they managed to fuse allegedly incompatible black and white styles while racial turmoil raged all around them.

"When a Man Loves a Woman" was Sledge's first recording of any kind, but lightning struck more than once. The follow-up release, **Warm and Tender Love**, was about as country as a soul singer could get without actually being Conway Twitty. **Out of Left Field** was a smouldering, powerful ballad that found Sledge reprising the atmosphere of "When a Man Loves a Woman". **Take Time to Know Her** was Sledge's second biggest hit and ranks as one of soul's great cautionary tales. Nowhere near as innovative as Otis Redding's version, Sledge's reading of **Try a Little Tenderness** showed just how close his style could be to white singers.

Sledge was best at grief, however. His version of **Drown in My Own Tears** doesn't have the bluesy exhaustion of Ray Charles's version; instead, Sledge sings it like he's writing a suicide note. His third single, **It Tears Me Up**, adhered to the standard Southern soul formula – clockwork percussion, dragging tempo, church organ, bleary horn interjections, twangy guitar punctuation – but his performance was anything but standard, portraying an anguish so deep that it makes you want to tear your hair out.

⟳We almost chose **Very Best of Percy Sledge**, Rhino, 1998

66

Sister Sledge

We Are Family

Cotillion, 1979

After Chic had basically bankrolled Atlantic for the next few years with 1978's *Le Freak*, main men Bernard Edwards and Nile Rodgers were offered the choice of producing anyone they wanted on Atlantic's roster. Like the iconoclasts they were, however, Chic picked a journeywomen girl group that barely had a hint of a hit during their five years at the label. Chic wanted to work with a group who didn't have an identity yet, but with Sister Sledge they didn't quite get a blank slate.

Kathie, Joni, Debra and Kim Sledge started recording as Sisters Sledge as teenagers in 1971. Based in Philadelphia, they released some material on the Money Back label and worked as backup singers for Gamble and Huff's Philadelphia International operation. As Sister Sledge, they signed to Atlantic in 1973 and had some success with "Love Don't Go Through No Changes on Me" in 1975, but for the most part they toiled in the background until Chic rescued them from obscurity. Recognising that in lead singer Kathie Sledge Sister Sledge had one of the most skilled vocalists in disco, Rodgers and Edwards subtly changed the standard Chic formula. Instead of crafting the strangely cryptic, ambivalent songs they did for Chic's female singers, Alfa Anderson and Luci Martin, Rodgers and Edwards gave Sister Sledge undeniably anthemic songs that downplayed Chic's disembodiment in favour of full-blooded disco-gospel release.

The first single from **We Are Family** was **He's the Greatest Dancer**. Led by an amazing, popping, almost slap-bass-sounding guitar figure from Rodgers, "He's the Greatest Dancer" became the group's first major hit, reaching the pop Top 10 and #1 on the R&B chart. The record featured some of the Chic Organization's best playing: Rodgers' guitar, Edwards' fluid bass-line, Tony Thompson's hard-hitting drums, Raymond Jones' best Fender Rhodes lines and some impeccable stuff from Concert Master Gene Orloff's Chic Strings. But it also highlighted Rodgers' and Edwards' songwriting prowess. Lines like "Arrogance, but not conceit/As a man he's complete" and the immortal internal rhyme, "Halston, Gucci, Fiorucci" were evidence of their gift for absurdist, plain-speech lyrics.

The album's best writing, however, was to be found on **Lost in Music**. It may not have been released as a single, but "Lost in Music" struck such a universal chord that it was covered fifteen years later by the cantankerous, Mancunian post-punk band the Fall – perhaps Sister Sledge's most unlikely admirers. Where Chic would have emphasised the "Caught in a trap/No turning back" part of the lyric with haunted vocals and deep spaces in the groove, Sister Sledge embody the "I feel so alive/I quit my nine to five" refrain with Kathie's swoops and curlicues and Rodgers' surging, uplifting chicken-scratch riffing.

For all of the brilliance of "Lost in Music", the album's biggest song was the title track. Based on a riff stolen from Children of God (a group that Rodgers admired when he was a hippy), **We Are Family** might have been a gospelesque get-happy tune about the joys of sisterhood, but it quickly became an all-purpose anthem used by everyone from feminists and gay rights activists to the Pittsburgh Pirates baseball team. There are other gems on the album, like the very fine disco love songs **You're a Friend to Me** and **Thinking of You**, but it was "We Are Family" that provided the conclusive proof of Chic's greatness (and helped win the World Series for the Pirates when they adopted it as their theme song).

⊃We almost chose **The Best of Sister Sledge (1973–1985)**, Rhino, 1992

67

Sly & the Family Stone

The Best of Sly & the Family Stone

Sony, 1992

The Beatles, the Rolling Stones, the Temptations and James Brown may have had more hits, but no one epitomised the late 1960s and early '70s more than Sly & the Family Stone. While other bands paid lip service to such '60s ideals as racial integration, sexual equality and fighting the establishment, the erstwhile Sylvester Stewart and his clan put the rhetoric into practice with some of the most radical, perfectly crafted, galvanising music ever.

Born March 15, 1941 in the outskirts of Dallas, Texas, Sylvester Stewart became the in-house producer at San Francisco's Autumn Records label in his early twenties. Originally crafting Bobby Freeman's dance craze hit, "C'mon and Swim", Stewart then went on to produce chart hits for white rock bands like the Beau Brummels and the Mojo Men. However, after attempting to rein in the chaos of psychedelic bands like the Warlocks (soon to become the Grateful Dead) and forcing Great Society (Grace Slick's first band) to do 200 takes of "Free Advice", Stewart got fed up with the Haight-Ashbury scene, changed his name to Sly Stone and created his own variant of psychedelia.

In order to create his fantasy world in which the libertarian axioms of Haight-Ashbury's white bohemia were actually applied to the struggle for Civil Rights, Sly recruited trumpeter Cynthia Robinson, sax player Jerry Martini, pianist Rosie Stone, guitarist Freddie Stone, drummer Greg Errico and bassist Larry Graham. The group's creation was an undeniable combination of stadium rock propulsion, gratuitous effects, proto-funk grooves and gospel-style positivity applied to the real world that made politics sound fun and fun sound like politics. While black nationalists were preaching separatism, the diverse racial make-up of the Family Stone made crossover seem like a political utopia. Perhaps even more radical was the crucial role women played as instrumentalists, not just vocal wallpaper to round out the band's sound.

Both gorgeous cacophony (**I Want to Take You Higher, Sing a Simple Song**) and perfectly crafted pop (**Everybody Is a Star, Hot Fun in the Summertime**), the band's music gave life to the greatest protest songs ever written. Sly's lyrics took pop's great subject, "everybody is a star", and made it a political statement of empowerment, belonging and belief. The messages were so strong that the band became a totem for the Woodstock nation and they tore the joint up at Yazgur's farm. The band's arrangements, which perfectly mirrored the lyrics, emphasised the variety of individual voices, both instrumental and vocal. While nearly all of soul's vocal groups grew out of the tradition of gospel harmonising, which featured tight ensemble singing and a defined lead singer, on tracks like **Dance to the Music** and **M'Lady** the Family Stone emphasised each group member's unique voice in arrangements that felt as if they were off the cuff and free-form even though they were obsessively produced down to the last detail.

By 1970, though, '60s idealism was dead and buried, and Sly reacted with one of pop music's most uncompromising moments: **Thank You (Falettinme Be Mice Elf Agin)** was a snarling vamp that was the group's most uncompromisingly funky record yet. Beginning with a vignette where Sly is wrestling with "the devil", "Thank You...." goes on to vent Sly's anger at his betrayal: "Thank you for the party, but I could never stay", "Dying young is hard to take, but selling out is harder". He then mocks the catch phrases of his old hits and, with the sardonic title phrase, the message was clear.

⮑We almost chose **Stand!**, Sony, 1969

68

Sly & the Family Stone

There's a Riot Goin' On

Epic, 1971

Sly & the Family Stone's early music was among the greatest music of the 1960s because it practised what it preached. A mixture of rock and soul, pop and funk, whites and blacks, men and women, Sly & the Family Stone represented the '60s dream made flesh. While the rock community paid lip service to tolerance and loving each other, the Family Stone were living it. The protest singers may have filled their songs with a self-righteousness that made their world a drag to live in, but the Family Stone made a joyful noise out of collectivity.

Then, after the decade's supposed zenith, it stopped. 1970's "Thank You (Falettinme Be Mice Elf Agin)" was a snarling record that intimated that Woodstock, and the group's triumph there, was a sham – "Thank you for the party, but I could never stay". Sly started failing to show up for concerts, he was wrestling with drug addiction, he was getting death threats and there were rumours that black nationalist leaders were trying to force him to make his music more radical. All of which meant that the group's new album was endlessly delayed. When **There's a Riot Goin' On** finally emerged in November 1971, the joy, the gorgeous mosaic of voices and the "different strokes for different folks" tolerance had vanished. In their places, were scorn, derision and dead spots so vast you felt like you'd just fallen off the end of the world. The deadest spot of all was the title track which clocked in at 0:00. While Marvin Gaye was making *What's Going On* as an article of faith in the power of pop music, Sly was highlighting his pessimism by sardonically pointing out that nothing whatsoever was going on.

There's a Riot Goin' On was probably the greatest music of the '70s because it also practised what it preached. "Feels so good inside myself, don't wanna move" was the album's opening line and its most joyous: the only time the album felt celebratory and one of the few moments when there are other voices aside from Sly's. The rest of *There's a Riot Goin' On*, cataloguing why Sly didn't want to move, was set to sketchy, slo-mo grooves too frugged to try to fight their way through the narcotic haze. Rarely have sound and vision been unified to such an extent.

At times listening to *There's a Riot Goin' On* is a bit like being stuck at a party with an incoherent drunk struggling not to pass out. When he's not gurgling and wailing like a hungry baby, Sly sings like he's talking to his chest. But, for all that, those odds and ends that you can make out from his mumble and the instrumental fog hit like a boot to the gut: "Out and down, ain't got a friend/Don't know who turned you in", "Time they say is the answer/But I don't believe it", "Dying young is hard to take, but selling out is harder".

The music feels just as incomplete as the lyrics, but perhaps only in comparison to the glorious overload of the group's old records. With its early use of a primitive drum machine, slow – really slow – tempos, scratchy guitar, one-note organ drones, deconstructed JB horn riffs and almost schematic bass-lines, *There's a Riot Goin' On* was Sly & the Family Stone in dub, or maybe in photo-negative. It was as precisely detailed as earlier albums like *I Want to Take You Higher* or *Dance to the Music*, only dragged through the ringer.

On subsequent albums, Sly may have retreated from such an uncompromising vision, but when you stare down the barrel of the gun and survive (sort of), there's nowhere else to go.

⊃We almost chose **Fresh**, Epic, 1973

69

Soul II Soul

Club Classics Vol. One

10/Virgin, 1989

It often seems that there are about one hundred people who listen to current R&B in Britain, a condition which tends to give the country's aspiring soul singers a perilous choice: stay trapped in a taste ghetto or produce crossover pap for middle-management types. With a combination of genius marketing, a good catch phrase, a couple of great tunes and innovative production, Soul II Soul actually managed to take its own agenda into the mainstream rather than being dictated to by it.

Soul II Soul was the baby of Beresford Romeo, aka Jazzie B, a first-generation Brit who was the son of Antiguan parents. After leaving school, Jazzie and Philip "Daddae" Harvey started the Soul II Soul sound system, which was modelled after the mobile DJ/dub crews of Jamaica. In 1985 they were hired by Bristol's Wild Bunch crew of DJs, producers and party throwers to bring their equipment for a London party. Jazzie and Harvey thought they were being hired as DJs and the misunderstanding escalated into a fight. However, in the way these things usually happen, the Wild Bunch's Nellee Hooper and Jazzie went to the pub, became friends, and Hooper joined Soul II Soul.

With a successful club night at Covent Garden's Africa Centre to their name, the group recorded a single, Fairplay, which was picked up by Virgin subsidiary 10 Records and reached the lower end of the UK's Top 100 in 1988. Engineered by future U2 collaborator Howie B, produced and arranged by Jazzie and Hooper and sung by Rose Windross,

"Fairplay" set out the Soul II Soul formula with tag-lines like "It's all about expression" leaping out from the jazzy keyboard washes. The follow-up single, Feel Free, featuring great Chic-style strings from the Reggae Philharmonic Orchestra, reached #63 in the UK charts, even though it was less focused and the sound never gelled.

But it was on their third single that everything came together to produce a Top 5 UK hit and an American R&B #1. Riding the beat from the Soul Searchers' "Ashley's Roach Clip", Keep On Movin' was one of those singles that immediately announce themselves as something great. Hooper's production (particularly the strings and the ghostly piano parts) reveal that he had been extensively studying the Chic songbook, while Caron Wheeler (who had been promoted from singing backup on "Feel Free") managed to make the British soul fan's obsession with jazzy oversinging into something more than bohemian irrelevance. In an R&B climate dominated by the likes of Atlantic Starr, Bobby Brown and Babyface, "Keep On Movin'" proved that you didn't have to be callow to have an R&B hit.

"Keep On Movin'" anchors Club Classics Vol. One, but it isn't the only standout. The great Back to Life is also here, but in its original a cappella form rather than the version issued as a single (their second R&B #1 in the US). When the drums do finally come in, they lead into Jazzie's Groove. Featuring what would become Soul II Soul's catch phrase ("A happy face, a thumpin' bass for a lovin' race"), "Jazzie's Groove" epito- mised the times, with its horn stabs and cut-up James Brown beat. As the Soul II Soul collective expanded to include fashion emporiums selling T-shirts, "A happy face . . ." threatened to become little more than a Frankie Goes to Hollywood-style slogan. But with the explosion of dance music in Britain at the time and the increasing visibility of Britain's black community, the catch phrase became more than a cheap marketing scam and was emblematic of the optimism that accompanied the end of Thatcherism.

⮌We almost chose **Vol. Two: 1990 – A New Decade**, 10, 1990

70

The Soul Stirrers

Sam Cooke with the Soul Stirrers

Specialty, 1991

The Soul Stirrers are unquestionably the most influential of all male harmony groups, secular or sacred, and quite possibly the greatest. Formed in 1927 in Trinity, Texas, the Soul Stirrers changed the face of gospel music in the mid-'30s when they changed their repertoire, and soon the repertoire of all harmony groups, from the traditional spirituals and jubilees to modern gospel compositions which were, until then, only sung in church. Even more revolutionary was the way the group shifted the vocal arrangements. Adding a second lead vocalist, the Soul Stirrers' brand-new style gave the first lead space for extended solo passages without abandoning the traditional harmony. This setup also created a contrast between the two lead voices, which enabled the group to crank up the emotional intensity and would soon become the stock in trade of every vocal group from the Swan Silvertones to the Temptations.

In gospel terms, the Soul Stirrers' most influential lead vocalist was R.H. Harris. Joining the group in 1936, Harris was responsible for most of the group's paradigm shifts in harmony group singing. Harris was a one-man quartet: he was perhaps the first sanctified falsetto singer, yet he could also growl with the best of them. Freed from the traditional harmony constrictions, Harris introduced blues-style ad-libs and jazzy syncopations to gospel singing, thus creating the archetype of the swooping, soaring, freestyling, sermonising gospel singer.

For soul aficionados, though, Harris's style was a bit too polished, a bit too elegant and a bit too old-world. The man who replaced Harris, however, practically invented soul singing. Recruited from the Soul Stirrers' farm team, the Highway Q.C.'s, Sam Cooke joined the Stirrers in 1950 and rewrote the gospel rule book once again. Cooke was 19 when he joined the group and his first recordings are noticeably rough around the edges and largely imitative of Harris. By 1953, though, on records like **Come and Go to That Land**, Cooke's characteristic smooth falsetto had fully developed. When he stretches out the word "go" to a "go-oahh-oahh", Cooke's trademark melismatic yodel was born and soul was just around the corner. A year later, Cooke's stunning vocal on **Any Day Now** was the blueprint for any number of doo-wop groups, particularly Harvey & the Moonglows.

With his graceful voice and square jaw, Cooke became gospel's first heart-throb. While the best gospel house-wreckers had always had a particularly strong effect on their female fans with their overwhelming emotion and powerful physicality, Cooke attracted legions of swooning teenagers. He became an accomplished showman and, with the success of songs like **Nearer to Thee** and **Wonderful**, Cooke had as many fan clubs as Clyde McPhatter. Cooke was no airheaded himbo, however: he wrote and arranged most of the Stirrers' material during his tenure. 1956's "Wonderful" was the big breakthrough: Cooke's singing now had a clarity and distinctly modern feel that was far removed from Harris's textbook style, and the instrumentation was so lush that it bordered on the sinful. Recorded at the same sessions, **Touch the Hem of His Garment** was even more secular in its arrangement. Ditching the harmony rule book, Cooke was firmly front and centre as the star, there was no second lead singer and the rest of the Stirrers had been relegated to a strictly background role. "Touch the Hem of His Garment" became a sizeable hit, making his conversion to pop singing inevitable.

➲We almost chose **Jesus Gave Me Water**, Specialty, 1992

71

Dusty Springfield

Dusty in Memphis

Mercury, 1995

Categories like "blue-eyed soul" tend to obscure the fact that soul, well at least Southern soul, was always the product of miscegenation. There are few better examples of this than Chips Moman's American Sound Studio in Memphis. Moman was a kid from rural Georgia who had formed an integrated band with Booker T. Jones in the late 1950s and had helped Jim Stewart at Stax during the label's early days before setting up his own studio in 1964. American used a band made up of mostly ex-country players (guitarist Reggie Young, bassist Tommy Cogbill, keyboardists Bobby Emmons and Bobby Wood and drummer Gene Chrisman) to cut soul sides by the likes of James and Bobby Purify, Joe Tex, Oscar Toney Jr., Roy Hamilton and Joe Simon. With American's success artists like Neil Diamond and Lulu started recording there and Atlantic brought down King Curtis and the Sweet Inspirations. Atlantic's biggest success with American Sound Studio was with Dusty Springfield.

Springfield was born Mary O'Brien in London in 1939. She began her career in the early '60s as part of the Springfields, a folk-pop trio she formed with her brother who had big hits like "Silver Thread and Golden Needles" before splitting just before the British Invasion. Going solo, she transformed herself into a gutsy vocalist and became, along with Dionne Warwick, the new generation's best interpreter of Brill Building pop material. Often credited as being a powerful soul singer, even on early records like "I Only Want to Be With You" and "Wishin' and

Hopin'", Springfield never sounded as credible or as powerful as she did on **Dusty in Memphis**.

Recorded at American with the studio's house band in 1968, *Dusty in Memphis* was easily the best album of her career and quite probably the best "blue-eyed soul" album ever. The album's key players – the 827 Thomas Street Band and backing vocalists the Sweet Inspirations – must take a lot of the credit. Although co-producer Arif Mardin gussied up the Memphis sound with Concert Master Gene Orloff's strings, the Al Jackson-inspired drums, the churchy keyboards, guitar slurs and the driving bass-lines ensure that enough barbecue grease drips from the arrangements. The Sweet Inspirations, meanwhile, take Springfield to church and inject a healthy bit of Raelets sass into the proceedings.

It all rubbed off on Springfield and, unlike many imports to Memphis, she doesn't sound out of place here. The funky, Memphis soul stew comes to the fore on **Son of a Preacher Man** and Springfield rides the groove for all it's worth. One of the most perfect matches between downhome values and mainstream pop sensibilities, "Son of a Preacher Man" was an American Top 10 hit and the album's signature song. Elsewhere, she breaks through her breathy mannerisms on **Don't Forget About Me**, comes on like a cross between Al Green and Bill Medley on **Breakfast in Bed** and has all the heartache of Lorraine Ellison on **I Can't Make It Alone**. Funky numbers like **Willie and Laura Mae Jones** and **That Old Sweet Roll (Hi-De-Ho)** were recorded at the same sessions, but were only released as singles or B-sides (but they are included here).

There are a few saccharine arrangements (**Just One Smile**) and some bad choices (**The Windmills of Your Mind**), but the pop impetus of the record anticipated some soul developments of the '70s. The electric sitar on **In the Land of Make Believe** must have given Gamble and Huff an idea or two, while the string melodrama might have been the genesis of Isaac Hayes' *Hot Buttered Soul*.

⤴We almost chose **The Silver Collection**, Philips, 1988

72

Donna Summer

Endless Summer

Polygram, 1994

Soul music is supposed to be all about *the voice* making the specific universal, turning pain into ecstasy and maybe even transcending the human condition altogether. With a couple of exceptions, though, soul is as much the sum of nearly interchangeable parts as any teenybop subgenre you care to name. Aside from maybe Motown, nowhere in the soul continuum is this more obvious than with Donna Summer. Disco is producer's music *par excellence* and with Donna Summer disco found its ultimate blank canvas.

Disco's naysayers criticise disco singers for having more in common with Broadway vocalists than with soul's more "authentic" expressionists. With Summer they've got a point: her phrasing wasn't all that different from Ethel Merman and even though she was supposed to have sung in church you sure couldn't find any evidence of it. In fact, Summer was an unknown singer from Boston who was in the Munich production of *Godspell* in 1974 when she met Giorgio Moroder. Moroder was a producer from the Tyrolian ski resort of Val Gardena until he happened across the Moog synthesizer at the dawn of the '70s. The Moog's distinctly space age timbres inspired Moroder to write "Son of My Father", which, in the hands of a group of slumming glam-rockers called Chicory Tip, became the first #1 record to feature a synthesizer. As glorious a piece of pop ephemera as "Son of My Father" was, however, Moroder was still a journeyman. With Summer and fellow producer Pete Bellotte, however, he defined the union of flesh and machine in dance music. Little more than Donna Summer simulating an orgasm over a background of blaxploitation cymbals, wah-wah guitars, a funky-butt clavinet riff and some synth chimes, Love to Love You Baby reached #2 in the American charts, but more importantly was largely responsible for the development of the 12" single.

Even more of a landmark was 1977's I Feel Love, with more fake-orgasm vocals from Summer set against an entirely synthesized background. Introducing both the syn-drum and the galloping Moog bass-line that would come to categorise the strain of disco called Hi-NRG, "I Feel Love" was a masterpiece of mechano-eroticism. Where synth-based records by Jean-Jacques Perrey, Kraftwerk, Tangerine Dream and Tonto's Expanding Head Band had used Moogs to imagine the whooshing speed and gurgling weirdness of a possible future, Moroder considered what implications the machine would have on the human body.

As Summer became a bigger and bigger star, however, Moroder and Bellotte backed away from the world of artifice towards a more conventional pop soundworld that featured massed strings and guitar solos from the likes of studio hack Jeff "Skunk" Baxter. While her version of MacArthur Park is as bad as any record Don Johnson or Bruce Willis ever made, Last Dance, On the Radio and Bad Girls belong on anyone's dance floor, and her duet with Barbra Streisand, No More Tears (Enough Is Enough), is camper than Nelson Eddy and Jeanette McDonald singing together in the shower.

Summer's greatest record, though, was made with Quincy Jones. With Summer singing the first two verses in a mock Puerto Rican accent to an electro-reggae lilt, 1982's State of Independence works from camp theatricality and kitsch exotica to the soaring emotion of reciprocated love and the orchestral grandeur of synthesised strings and gospel chorus. Like "I Feel Love", "State of Independence" was a synth masterpiece that revelled in artifice, and if that's not transcending the human condition, I don't know what is.

⮑We almost chose **On the Radio: Greatest Hits**, Casablanca, 1979

Diana Ross & the Supremes

The Ultimate Collection

Motown, 1997

Saying that Motown belched out prefabricated product with the same regularity as Ford's Red River plant churned out Fairmonts is to neglect the divergent styles of, say, Smokey Robinson's simple, singsong arrangements for the Temptations and Holland-Dozier-Holland's whirlpools of sound for the Four Tops. What Motown offered was an instantly recognisable sound, inch-perfect craftsmanship and a seemingly endless repertoire of hooks and catch phrases. Whatever parallels may be drawn with the neighbouring automobile production lines, Motown was a lot more than an unlikely commercial juggernaut. It was the ultimate symbol of black economic self-sufficiency. At the same time, it represented the integrationist ideal: articulating the black bourgeoisie's claim on the American Dream by courting a white audience without diluting African-American culture. Of course, the music also spoke on its own terms as perfectly crafted pop. As a mediator in countless romances, as a new rhapsodic language, as the voice of unarticulated pleasure and loss, it was, as the label claimed, "the sound of young America".

If there was a Motown act that epitomised the label as "the sound of young America", it was the Supremes. During the 1960s only the Beatles were more successful and Michael Jackson is the only black artist to achieve more pop #1s. Like Jackson, however, the Supremes were more successful on the pop chart than they were on the R&B chart. Motown founder Berry Gordy wanted nothing more than to belong to the establishment and the Supremes were his meal ticket. Astringent and overly stylised, Diana Ross wasn't that great a pop singer, much less a mediocre R&B singer. The reason that this CD belongs in this book is because of what's going on behind the scenes and underneath the vocals.

Until 1968, when they left Motown to start their own label, the Supremes were produced by the team of Brian Holland, Lamont Dozier and Eddie Holland, who would go on to become possibly the greatest production team in the history of pop music. At Motown, the H-D-H team created monumental records for the Four Tops ("I Can't Help Myself", "Reach Out I'll Be There", "Bernadette", "Standing in the Shadows of Love"), Martha and the Vandellas ("Nowhere to Run", "Heat Wave"), Marvin Gaye ("Can I Get a Witness"), Junior Walker ("(I'm a) Road Runner"), Mary Wells ("You Lost the Sweetest Boy") and Smokey Robinson & the Miracles ("I Gotta Dance to Keep From Crying"), in addition to the Supremes. With the aid of the Motown studio band, the Funk Brothers, H-D-H made huge, crashing records that, although filled with detail and nuance, relied on sheer force for their effectiveness. Crucially, H-D-H understood the link between cars, freedom, teenage lust and music. As a result, their enormous sound was EQ'd to breaking point and aimed directly at the tiny, tinny speakers of car audio where much of the emotional life of young America was played out.

Listen to Supremes records like Where Did Our Love Go, Come See About Me, Stop! In the Name of Love, You Can't Hurry Love, You Keep Me Hangin' On and Love Is Like an Itching in My Heart on small, low-fidelity speakers and the art becomes clear. Ross's thin vocals are surrounded by insistent, simple guitar riffs that anticipate reggae, 21-horn salutes, bells and James Jamerson's huge bass undertow. While Ross's voice doesn't crack with the emotional intensity the lyrics deserve, the music does, and that's what soul is all about.

⟳We almost chose **Anthology**, Motown, 1995

Swamp Dogg

Total Destruction of Your Mind/Rat On

Charly, 1991

A legend on the British "deep soul" scene, Jerry Williams Jr. is one of the most original talents to ever cut a soul side. As a producer, Williams has been responsible for good-to-great records by C & the Shells, the Exciters, Charlie & Inez Foxx, Gary US Bonds, Irma Thomas and, most famously, Doris Duke. It's his records as Swamp Dogg, however, that ensure Williams a place in the soul pantheon. Alongside Norman Whitfield's productions for the Temptations, Sly Stone and George Clinton's Parliafunkadelicment Thang, Swamp Dogg was responsible for expanding soul's parameters in the early 1970s. In many ways, he was probably the most radical of them all.

Born in Portsmouth, Virginia in 1942, Williams was raised in a musical family that included stepfather guitarist Nat Cross and local drummer Miss Vera. His unique take on soul can perhaps be traced to his Catholic upbringing, which meant that he didn't have the usual gospel training or grounding in tradition of most soul singers. Williams recorded his first record in 1954 as a 12-year-old, calling himself Little Jerry. By the time he was 18, he had written a book of poetry, two plays, a novel and produced a local TV show. After a decade as a journeyman producer and singer, he came up with the Swamp Dogg persona as a reaction to the standard packaging formulas of the record industry. As outrageous as George Clinton, as in-your-face as a punk Little Richard and as down and dirty as Dyke & the Blazers, Swamp Dogg was what Otis Redding might have sounded like if he had dropped acid with the "love crowd" after Monterey and stayed with them through the disillusionment of the Chicago Democratic Convention and the Kent State Massacre.

Originally released on Canyon Records in 1970, **Total Destruction of Your Mind** was fairly typical Southern soul in the Stax/Muscle Shoals mould, with a rougher edge and a bit more drive. Like the music, his voice was as raw as you could imagine; Robert Christgau has described it as "an Afro-American air raid siren". The album's big hit was a blues ditty called Mama's Baby, Daddy's Maybe, in which the singer's wife gives birth to a baby with blue eyes that's "a little brighter, a wee bit lighter than anybody in our families". It was in the classic cheating song vein, but the details subtly subverted the form and gave the song a dimension no one else would have dared broach.

Williams was one of the few soul artists to openly take on the establishment (check Raw Spitt's incredible "Songs to Sing", which Williams wrote and produced on *Dave Godin's Deep Soul Treasures Volume 1*), and *Total Destruction*'s triumph is that the message comes across loud and clear without being cloying or crass. Instead of couching his rage in biblical metaphors, Swamp Dogg tackled racism as confrontationally as Stokely Carmichael. His version of Joe South's Redneck is likely the most daring song ever recorded by a black singer, while his own I Was Born Blue is one of the most moving.

Total Destruction was a cause célèbre among hip soul fans and the press reaction helped get the Dogg signed to Elektra. His only album for the label was 1971's **Rat On**. Although *Rat On* couldn't recapture *Total Destruction*'s inspired lunacy, it did feature two songs as remarkable as anything on *Total Destruction*. God Bless America, For What brought a suit from the Irving Berlin Foundation for using the name of Berlin's song in vain, while Remember I Said Tomorrow was the best indictment of political hypocrisy that Bob Dylan never wrote.

⭮We almost chose **Gag a Maggot Stone**, Dogg, 1973

Swan Silvertones

Love Lifted My/Me Rock

Specialty, 1991

Along with the Soul Stirrers, the Swan Silvertones were the greatest of the male gospel harmony groups. Until he quit the group in the mid-1960s, the Silvertones' leader was Claude Jeter, probably the greatest singer you've never heard of and the undisputed godfather of falsetto. Like all great vocal groups, the Swan Silvertones worked on contrast and Jeter's foils were the amazing shouters Solomon Womack and Rev. Robert Crenshaw. While Jeter was controlled and smooth, there have never been any other singers as intense and febrile and raggedy as Womack and Crenshaw. The broken glass–honey approach of the Swan Silvertones made them the ultimate house-wreckers and the model for any number of soul vocal groups, particularly the Temptations.

The Swan Silvertones had their origins in Jeter's first group, the Four Harmony Kings, which he founded in 1938 while working in the coal mines of West Virginia. During World War II the group was offered a spot on a radio station in Tennessee sponsored by Swan Bakery. The group, by this time including longtime baritone John Myles, changed their name to the Swan Silvertones. Womack joined just before they made their first recordings for the King label in 1945. Over the next six years, they recorded 45 sides for the label, including "I Bowed My Knees and Cried Holy", which was one of the main transition records between the Jubilee style of groups like the Golden Gate Quartet and the modern style of the Silvertones and the Soul Stirrers.

In 1951 the Silvertones – Jeter, Womack, Myles, Crenshaw, John Manson and Henry Bossard – moved to Specialty, for whom they recorded some of their best work. The following year Paul Owens, a gospel veteran who learned his craft with the Dixie Hummigbirds, came on board and, with his arrangements and elegant leads, turned the group into the most popular gospel group of the next two decades. This reissue of their two albums for Specialty contains most of the sides the group recorded between 1951 and 1955 before they moved to Vee-Jay. In tandem with the Soul Stirrers' records with Sam Cooke, these are songs that changed the face of popular music and are the most important gospel records for secular fans.

One of the most staggering vocal performances ever caught on vinyl, Jeter's version of **I'm Coming Home** might be the perfect gospel record: it's got that unique combination of unbearable sadness and ecstasy, of existential dread and salvation, that allows the best gospel to transcend the ghetto of faith that imprisons much religious music. This is why gospel became the model for most postwar popular music and "I'm Coming Home" encapsulates the twenty years of African-American music that followed: doo-wop, the Impressions, Maurice & the Zodiacs, the Stylistics, Al Green.

With singers as desperate as Womack and Crenshaw, the Silvertones could also exorcise demons with uncanny ferocity. The snapped-diaphragm intensity of James Brown and the stomping release of rock'n'roll can be traced to Silvertones upsetters like **Trouble in My Way** and **How I Got Over**. With bass singer Henry Bossard moving his mouth like Jimmy Blanton, a swinging beat and Crenshaw testifying like his life depends on it, "My Rock" is probably their most famous screamer and is as cathartic as any record made by the Ramones or Bad Brains or Metallica or NWA. The only problem with the Swan Silvertones is that their music is so great, it nearly eclipses the glories they're singing about.

➲We almost chose **Swan Silvertones/Singin' In My Soul**, Vee-Jay, 1993

Sylvester

Star: The Best of Sylvester

Southbound/Ace, 1989

In a just world Sylvester would be as big as Michael Jackson or Prince. With his flamboyance, shimmer, sexual charisma and fierce high-energy beats, Sylvester is everything pop music is meant to be. Aside from Chic and the NYC Peech Boys, no one else of his time seemed to recognise that the disco was both utopia and hell – the tension from which all truly great dance music is born. Most significantly, however, his use of his gospel-trained falsetto in the service of gay desire is surely the most radical rewrite of pop's lingua franca ever attempted.

Sylvester James was born in 1947 and, like most singers of his generation, learned his craft in church. By his teens, the music of Bessie Smith and Billie Holiday had supplanted gospel, and when he moved to San Francisco in the late '60s he starred in a cabaret show called "Women of the Blues". In 1970 he joined the cross-dressing revue troupe the Cockettes and quickly became an underground star. When he began his solo career in 1973 with Sylvester and the Hot Band, he was covering Neil Young and James Taylor, and he continued down this rock path until he hooked up with former Moonglow Harvey Fuqua in 1977.

With Fuqua, Sylvester moved in a more soul-oriented direction and their first album together, *Sylvester,* produced one solid disco floor-burner and an all-time classic (both of which are included here). Down, Down, Down was pretty formulaic first-wave disco and the workmanlike arrangement made Sylvester's voice sound weak, but it did have energy and pace and the song became a modest club hit in New York. It was a version of Nickolas Ashford and Valerie Simpson's Over and Over, though, that propelled Sylvester towards disco superstardom. Rather than the dance-floor heat with which he would become associated, "Over and Over" was a guitar-and-bass slow-burn whose intensity came from impassioned vocals by Sylvester and his great backup singers, Izora Rhodes and Martha Wash.

Following this somewhat limited success, 1978's *Step II* brought Sylvester temporarily into the mainstream. The album's first single, Dance (Disco Heat), was a fairly mindless, but irresistible disco bounce-along that featured Rhodes and Wash (now known as Two Tons o' Fun) and reached the American Top 20. Although the follow-up, You Make Me Feel (Mighty Real), barely creeped into the US Top 40, it is Sylvester's greatest record. With its synth licks, mechanised bass-line and drum-machine beats, the song is the genesis of the disco subgenre known as Hi-NRG. Usually little more than an aural fantasy of a futuristic club populated entirely by cybernetic Tom of Finland studs, the Hi-NRG created by Sylvester, Fuqua and synth player Patrick Cowley interrogated the African-American musical tradition and asked what "realness" is supposed to mean to gay, black men forced to hide their true identities for most of their lives.

After "You Make Me Feel (Mighty Real)", Cowley began to play a bigger role in Sylvester's music (eventually becoming his producer in the '80s) and he penned 1979's Stars (Everybody Is One). With similar, but not as immediate, production as "You Make Me Feel (Mighty Real)", "Stars" was a celebration of disco's fantasy world, where everyone could be what they wanted to be despite the "immutable" laws of biology. Tracks like Body Strong and his cover of Ben E. King's I (Who Have Nothing) continued in the same vein, and Sylvester's union of flesh, emotion and machine reinforced his status as the ultimate disco star.

⮌We almost chose **Greatest Hits: Non-Stop Dance Party**, Fantasy, 1983

77

Howard Tate

Get It While You Can: The Legendary Sessions

Mercury, 1995

Although Rudy Van Gelder's studio in his living room in suburban Englewood Cliffs, New Jersey is sacred ground in jazz circles, it hardly resonates with the mythopoetic force of Chips Moman's American Sound Studio for soul fans. Nonetheless, in the person of Howard Tate, this unlikely locale, right across the river from the stronghold of uptown soul and Brill Building pop, produced some of the greatest deep soul sides ever.

Howard Tate is a bit of a mystery man. Even the legions of European soul obsessives who have dug up every possible biographical detail about the most obscure artists have been stymied in their efforts to track down Tate. What is known is that Tate was born in Macon, Georgia in 1938 and spent his formative years in Philadelphia, where he whiled away his adolescence doo-wopping with Garnet Mimms. In the early '60s he was the lead singer for Bill Doggett's band. Other than that, his life before and after these "legendary sessions" is pretty sketchy. What remains most mysterious about Tate, though, is how did a man who spent most of his life above the Mason-Dixon line get such an affinity for downhome sounds?

Recorded in April 1966, Tate's debut single, **Ain't Nobody Home**, was released in June by the Verve label and became Tate's biggest hit, reaching #12 on the R&B chart and #63 pop. With a groove laid down by keyboardist Richard Tee, guitarist Cornell Dupree, bassist Chuck Rainey and drummer Herb Lovell, the production of "Ain't Nobody Home" (by

Jerry Ragavoy) both borrowed from and influenced the music coming from Memphis and Muscle Shoals and set the precedent for Atlantic's first recordings with Aretha Franklin. While the music was great, however, it was Tate that made the record. Sounding like a less overwrought Percy Sledge, Tate's phrasing was impeccable and the economic use of his falsetto made it that much more effective. The B-side was a cover of Lorraine Ellison's "How Come My Bulldog Don't Bark" and the rumbling blues arrangement tipped off careful listeners that his sound was as rooted in B.B. King as it was in Otis Redding.

The follow-up, Look At Granny Run Run, was a Mort Shuman throwaway, but did almost as well on the charts as "Ain't Nobody Home". Tate's third single, Get It While You Can, was another Shuman/Ragavoy collaboration and sounded like it came straight out of west Tennessee. The bleary horns and comping guitar screamed Memphis, while Tate outdid Solomon Burke in the secular-preacher-of-love stakes. Despite being an archetypal soul record, it failed to make an impression on the charts until Janis Joplin got hold of it. More near-perfect churchy soul followed in the form of I Learned It All the Hard Way, but it too failed to dent the charts.

Despite his affinity for sermonising, Tate's best record was "Stop". Perfecting the sound that Ragavoy had constructed on "Ain't Nobody Home", "Stop" was an infectious groove created from the greatest non-Memphis piano line ever and a horn-arranging masterclass given by Garry Sherman. And, once again, with his restrained but emotional melisma, Tate stole the show. Tate's blues-based economy was so effective that "Stop" would later be covered by both Jimi Hendrix and Hugh Masekela.

Tate failed to have any hits after "Stop", however, and he was dropped by Verve. He recorded a few singles and an album for Lloyd Price's Turntable label in the early '70s, but he has virtually disappeared from the scene since then.

⮑We almost chose **Reaction**, Turntable, 1981

78

The Temptations

Anthology

Motown, 1995

From the almost naive sweetness of their early records with Smokey Robinson to the dark paranoia of their later records with Norman Whitfield, the Temptations were certainly Motown's most versatile and probably best vocal group. Unlike the Supremes, with whom they're often paired, the Temptations were modelled on the classic harmony-group foundation laid down by gospel groups like the Soul Stirrers and the Swan Silvertones. With David Ruffin's rough-hewn leads and Eddie Kendricks' floating falsetto, the Temptations had two of soul's finest and most recognisable vocalists.

The Temptations cut their first record with Motown in 1962, but it wouldn't be until 1964, when David Ruffin joined Kendricks, Otis Williams, Paul Williams and Melvin Franklin, that they had their first hit. With an almost singsong arrangement and hokey lines like "The way you swept off my feet, you could have been a broom/You smell so sweet, you could have been perfume", the group's first hit, The Way You Do the Things You Do, was pure Smokey Robinson, but the Temptations became Robinson's best vehicle because only singers as talented as Ruffin and Kendricks could ride the jaunty melody and give it any sort of conviction. With its sublime melody, perfect arrangement and instantly memorably bass and finger-snap breakdown, perhaps anyone could have sung My Girl and made it a hit, but Ruffin's swoops and the group's harmonies made it such an enduring pop shibboleth.

The Tempts continued to have hits with Robinson (the dramatic Since I Lost My Baby and Get Ready), but with Ain't Too Proud to Beg the group was shifted to Norman Whitfield. Whitfield is one of the greatest producers in the history of pop music, as his records with the Tempts testify. From the intro, which has Ruffin rasping over a sanctified, Holy Roller beat (this was just about the churchiest Motown ever got), to the "chank"ing guitar to Whitfield's prostrate lyrics, "Ain't Too Proud to Beg" was a whole new sound for the group that emphasised their gospel roots.

After the slight Beauty Is Only Skin Deep, the Tempts' next big hit was one of the calling cards of paranoid soul. (I Know) I'm Losing You began with an ominous guitar line that set the stage for the roiling horns and Ruffin's amazing portrayal of overwhelming jealousy. This paranoia would become Whitfield's signature sound. Ruffin left the group in 1968 and, with the loss of the group's most distinctive singer, Whitfield brought in Detroit session guitarist Dennis Coffey and his wah-wah pedal, and created dark, noisy, funky music, dubbed "psychedelic soul", for the Tempts on tracks like Cloud Nine, Runaway Child, Running Wild, Don't Let the Joneses Get You Down, Psychedelic Shack, Ball of Confusion and the towering I Can't Get Next to You.

Whitfield let up on the crybabies and flangers for 1971's Just My Imagination (Running Away With Me). It might have been a wimpy retro-doo-wop number, but it still dealt with the same sense of confusion that marked the best Whitfield records. Whitfield was up to his old tricks, however, with what might be his and the group's finest moment, Papa Was a Rolling Stone. With a bass-line that was more like a black hole than a groove, a fenetic wah-wah guitar part and just about the most dramatic arrangement imaginable, "Papa" was a seering interrogation of black masculine stereotypes. "Papa" was impossible to follow up, but just for good measure on "The Law of the Land" Whitfield would create a mechanised beat that was the birthplace of disco.

⮑We almost chose **Emperors of Soul**, Motown, 1994

Joe Tex

His Greatest Hits

Charly, 1996

Although they are often viewed as diametric opposites, soul and country music are really flip-sides of the same coin and the two genres have greatly influenced one another. With his hillbilly nickname and trademark ten-gallon Stetson hat, Joe Tex was perhaps the most obvious musician to blur this generic and racial boundary. Like many soul singers (Al Green, Ray Charles, Isaac Hayes, to name a few), Tex was a fan of Hank Williams and he actually wanted to be a country singer. Despite the fact that many country artists were taught how to play by black musicians, Tex was unable to cross country's colour barrier, and became a soul singer. Ironically, Tex's producer, Buddy Killen, was one of Nashville's biggest music publishers and Tex's songs have since been covered by country stars like Johnny Cash and Barbara Mandrell. Perhaps the biggest irony was that while the erstwhile Joseph Arrington Jr. wanted nothing more than to play the *Grand Ole Opry*, his legacy is as one of the definitive Southern soul artists.

Joe Tex's biggest influence was actually the black church. He utilised the homilies and hosannas of the black preacher to such an extent that he was the first soul singer to be nicknamed "The Rapper". After almost a decade of trying, Tex's first hit was little more than a sermon about fidelity over a dragging beat, bleary horn charts and a wheezy organ. Hold What You've Got was Southern soul's first big crossover hit, reaching #5 in 1964. Although it was Southern soul's calling card, "Hold What You've Got" was atypical of the style. Unlike the now-familiar emotionalism of artists like Otis Redding and Sam & Dave, Tex hardly sang at all after the introduction, opting instead for the measured cadences of a minister preaching to his congregation. With the exception of the archetypal horn arrangement, the shuffling music similarly had more to do with early rock'n'roll ballads than with the punchy rhythms of Southern soul.

With his solemn, preachy style, Tex's next several hits were, perhaps inevitably, more testaments to faithfulness. **I Want to (Do Everything For You)** actually had Tex singing, but it still couldn't escape the rhythms of the church with the answering chorus and Tex's dramatic punctuations. His second R&B #1, **A Sweet Woman Like You**, was another homiletic track that managed to bring in a touch of melody. More original, though, were his message tracks. **Don't Make Your Children Pay (For Your Mistakes)**, **A Woman's Hands** and, especially, **The Love You Save (May Be Your Own)** were all pure down-home preaching, patronising, paternalistic, but unlike anything else in the soul canon.

Pretty soon, though, Tex's sermons stopped hitting the charts and he resorted to recording novelty songs. Moody, stretched-out and deeply, deeply funky, **Papa Was Too** was Tex's entry into the "Tramp" saga started by Lowell Fulson. **Show Me** was countrified Motown dripping with barbecue grease, while **Skinny Legs and All** combined girl-watching, locker-room humour, Tex's preaching and patriarchy in one ridiculously catchy package. The biggest hit of Tex's career, though, was 1971's preposterously funky creation **I Gotcha**.

After a three-year hiatus from recording during which time he converted to Islam and proselytised for the black Muslims, Tex returned with another novelty record, 1976's disco smash, **Ain't Gonna Bump No More (With No Big Fat Woman)**. He continued in the same vein for the rest of his career, writing and recording songs about getting corns on his feet and the like, but just how bad can records be with titles like **You Might Be Diggin' the Garden (But Somebody's Picking Your Plums)** and Finger Popped Myself Into the Poor House?

⊃ We almost chose **The Very Best of Joe Tex**, Rhino, 1996

Irma Thomas

Sweet Soul Queen of New Orleans: The Irma Thomas Collection

Razor & Tie, 1996

While producer extraordinaire Allen Toussaint is primarily known for his Carnival sound records with Ernie K-Doe, Lee Dorsey and the Meters, his most emotive, and perhaps most soulful, records were made with Irma Thomas. Like many of America's great songwriters, arrangers and producers, Toussaint wrote songs specifically for each artist's individual voice. In Thomas he found a singer who was perhaps the perfect transition figure between R&B and soul: Thomas's voice had as much blues in it as gospel, she was more rhythmically dextrous than most female singers of the day and she was just as effective doing a slow smoulder as she was on the more breathless, uptempo numbers. Thus, with Thomas, Toussaint crafted deep, dark records that were the antithesis of the Crescent City's party-hearty reputation.

Irma Thomas was born in February 1941 in Ponchatoula, Louisiana, but by the time she was 14 she was living in New Orleans and was pregnant with her first child. Four years later, she was married for the second time, had three kids and was working as a waitress at the Pimloco Club in New Orleans, which was the residence of Tommy Ridgley's band. One night she persuaded him to let her sing and blew away both the crowd and Ridgley. A week later she was recording her first record with Ridgley for Joe Ruffino's Ron label. The result, the bluesy "You Can Have My Husband, Don't Mess With My Man" (not included here), was a modest R&B hit, but she wouldn't really hit her stride until she started to record for Minit Records and Allen Toussaint.

Thomas started working with Toussaint in 1961, and the first release was the sublime Cry On. Although the record went nowhere, "Cry On" was nearly perfect: a lachrymose organ and a drunken rhythm section set the backing for Thomas defeated, but very sexy, vocals. On 1963's It's Raining, Thomas again made Toussaint seem like a genius by giving depth to a fairly standard rock'n'roll ballad arrangement. "It's Raining" was a huge hit in her hometown, but again it failed to garner any national attention.

It wasn't all doom and gloom, however. On Hittin' on Nothing, Thomas was as tough and sassy as any female singer around, while on I Done Got Over It she gave some restrained gospel oomph to one of Toussaint's trademark, comic Mardi Gras beats. Her best record with Minit, however, was Ruler of My Heart, which took the ancient New Orleans second-line rhythm on a journey through a cold night of the soul. One quarter churchy devotional hymn, one quarter bayou hoodoo, one quarter lovelorn torture, one quarter barroom blues, "Ruler of My Heart" was such a devastating record that Otis Redding re-recorded it as "Pain in My Heart" and brought the song to its rightful place in the pop charts.

Towards the end of 1963, Toussaint was drafted into the army and Minit rapidly foundered. Thomas then went out to LA and recorded for Imperial Records. Working with producer H.B. Barnum, she finally had a national hit in 1964 with the self-penned Wish Someone Would Care. The dragging drums and funereal bell peals couldn't have been further away from her New Orleans sound, but the atmosphere combined with her own ravaged vocals to create a devastating anthem of self-pity. To add insult to an obviously already injured psyche, her follow-up single, "Time Is On My Side", was copied note for note by the Rolling Stones and became their first American hit, while Thomas's version, and her subsequent chart career, unjustly stalled.

⊃We almost chose **Time Is On My Side**
(The Best of Irma Thomas), EMI, 1992

81

War

All Day Music

Rhino, 1971

Of all the bands to come from Los Angeles, War probably came closest to embodying all the diverse images of the City of Angels – Hollywood glamour, endless beaches, palm-lined streets paved with gold, smog, one huge faceless suburb, Third World melting pot boiling over with racial strife. War was formed out of the ashes of a local group called the Creators when superstar defensive lineman for the LA Rams, Deacon Jones, was looking for a backing band as he tried his hand at singing. Hooking up a year later with former Animals lead singer Eric Burdon, War backed him for two albums, producing the hits "Spill the Wine" and "They Can't Take Away Our Music".

In 1971 guitarist Howard Scott, bassist B.B. Dickerson, keyboardist Lonnie Jordan, drummer Harold Brown, percussionist Papa Dee Allen, horn player Charles Miller and Danish harmonica ace Lee Oskar got rid of Burdon and grabbed the spotlight for themselves. Their first album, *War*, was pretty average and didn't do much, but their second album, **All Day Music**, established the group as one of the most important funk troupes of the '70s. Picking up on one of the underappreciated currents of SoCal music, War concocted a potent blend of funk rhythms, rock force, harmony-group vocal chops and Latin accents. Simultaneously joyful and frugged, War sounded like a group of community activists brushing the smoke from the Watts riots out of their eyes. Unlike too many politically aware bands, however, War never forgot that pleasure has its own dialectic and their grooves spoke as emphatically as their lyrics.

Like such heroes of the avant-garde as Teo Macero (who worked on Miles Davis's '70s recordings) and Krautrock funka-teers Can, War producer Jerry Goldstein often edited down tapes of the band jamming in order to conjure "songs" from the instrumental morass. *All Day Music*'s title cut was born in this way. A slow and lazy ode to relaxation, **All Day Music** could be an Angeleno version of the Small Faces' "Itchycoo Park", with its Afro-Cuban percussion, salsa-flavoured keyboards, spaghetti western harmonica and smooth harmonies.

While it maintained the same hazy groove, *All Day Music* got considerably less daydreamy quickly. The album's second track, **Get Down**, may have been titled like an airheaded invitation to boogie, but its real intentions were soon clear. The outrage of the lyrics ("Police and the justice laughing while they bust us") was matched by the seething menace of the percolating drum and bass groove. **That's What Love Will Do** followed with the spaced-out tale of a paranoid lover and more gloomy funk passages that sounded like they were dragging their feet behind them. When **There Must Be a Reason** emerged from the fog with lines like "Lost my soul in '68, where were you?", it became clear that "That's What Love Will Do" is part of the African-American tradition of channelling political aggression into love songs. Not even a group as courageous as War – who often got threats from the police for performing "Get Down" live – could openly say what they trying to express on "That's What Love Will Do" and "There Must Be a Reason".

Nappy Head combined Santana-esque guitars, conga fills, *güiro* patterns, montuno piano and voices in the crowd yelling "Viva La Raza", to create a Latino version of the soundtrack to Melvin Van Peebles' original blaxploitation flick, *Sweet Sweetback's Baadasss Song – ¡Sabroso!* "Nappy Head" led into the album's masterpiece, **Slippin' Into Darkness**, a dark, dubby track that stares into the heart of the spiritual dissolution of America and deserves to be ranked alongside "There's a Riot Goin' On", "Papa Was a Rolling Stone" and "Back Stabbers".

⊃We almost chose **Anthology**, Rhino, 1994

82

Billy Ward & the Dominoes

Sixty Minute Man

King, 1990

Of all the early rock'n'roll vocal groups who would have a profound impact on the direction of soul music, the Dominoes were perhaps the greatest. In the persons of Clyde McPhatter and Jackie Wilson, they were certainly blessed with the two best vocalists of the period, and with the talent-spotting and commercial instincts of group leader Billy Ward, the Dominoes became a hitmaking machine during the 1950s.

Billy Ward was born in Los Angeles in 1921 and by the time he had formed the Dominoes in 1950, he had been a classically trained soprano singer, a choir singer, a boxer, a soldier, a journalist and a voice teacher. In 1950 Ward heard Clyde McPhatter singing tenor with the gospel group, the Mount Lebanon Singers, and persuaded him to join the Dominoes. Along with McPhatter, Ward recruited second tenor Charlie White, baritone singer Joe Lamont and bass singer Bill Brown, and the Dominoes were signed to King's new R&B subsidiary Federal in 1950. The group's first release, **Do Something For Me/Chicken Blues**, featured McPhatter's sinfully beautiful singing and rose to #6 on the R&B charts.

It would be the Dominoes' third single, however, that would forever enshrine them in the annals of popular music. **Sixty Minute Man** was not only the biggest R&B hit of 1951, but it also reached #23 on the pop charts, making them the first of the new breed of vocal groups to cross over the secular River of Jordan. The irony was that "Sixty Minute Man" wasn't sung by

McPhatter, but the group's bass singer, Bill Brown. Arranged by Ward, "Sixty Minute Man" helped inaugurate the trend of soul music to combine the utterly salacious with the heavenly.

More great proto-rock'n'roll followed in the shape of the wailing That's What You're Doing to Me and "Deacon Moves In", which featured Little Esther Phillips. It would be 1952's Have Mercy Baby, however, that would be the Dominoes' true legacy to soul. With McPhatter using his gospel melisma with Holy Roller fervour and then breaking out in sobs at the end, "Have Mercy Baby" was the first secular record to rock with all-out sanctified frenzy. The Bells, on the other hand, was one of those slow, mournful hymns that would make Mahalia Jackson's name. "The Bells" was no age-old spiritual, however. With McPhatter breaking into histrionics and pitiful sobs, it could only have been further away from Jackson's stately grace if it was sung by Ozzy Osbourne. On records like the gorgeous Don't Leave Me This Way, McPhatter shelved his over-the-top emotionalism in favour of a piercing tenor that would be imitated on countless doo-wop records. Meanwhile, his nasal shouting on I'd Be Satisfied laid the groundwork for Jackie Wilson.

In fact, when McPhatter left the group in 1953, he was replaced by Wilson. You Can't Keep a Good Man Down was Wilson's first record with the group, now billed as Billy Ward & the Dominoes. Wilson's slightly astringent sound was obviously influenced by McPhatter, but Wilson also brought an operatic range and sense of melodrama, which Ward capitalised on by moving away from the rousing R&B of their earlier records. While records like "I'm Gonna Move to the Outskirts of Town" were sufficiently bluesy and showed off Wilson's stunning range and crystal falsetto, it was only a short step away from the versions of overripe standards like "Rags to Riches", "St. Therese of the Roses", "Star Dust" and "When the Swallows Come Back to Capistrano" (thankfully, none of which are included here) that would characterise the group's final period.

⮌We almost chose **Sixty Minute Men**, Rhino, 1993

83

Dionne Warwick

The Dionne Warwick Collection

Rhino, 1989

Certainly the only artist in this book with even the faintest connection to Marlene Dietrich, Dionne Warwick brought soul into the suburbs. Motown might have hooked kids with disposable incomes cruising in their cars, but Warwick's versions of Bacharach-David songs appealed to their leisure apparel-clad parents as well. With the sharp, piercing, intricate arrangements of Burt Bacharach, the almost-Cole Porter zing of Hal David's wordplay and her own supper-club soft-gospel vocals, Warwick's early records marked the shift between R&B and soul and laid the groundwork for soul's mainstream crossover.

Born in New Jersey in 1940, Marie Dionne Warwick formed a gospel trio, the Gospelaires, with her sister Dee Dee and her aunt Cissy Houston in the '50s. At the end of the decade she began a career as a studio backup singer and was picked out of the crowd by the former arranger for Marlene Dietrich's cabaret act, Burt Bacharach, when she sang on the Drifters' "Mexican Divorce" in 1961. As the anointed voice for Bacharach-David productions, Warwick would score 22 American Top 40 hits over the following decade under the duo's aegis.

Warwick's first hit was 1962's Don't Make Me Over. Not only a commercial success, it was an artistic triumph as she managed not to drown in the string undertow and, along with singers like Maxine Brown and Baby Washington, showed the way for female pop singers to escape the shackles of the girl-group sound. Toning the melodrama down a bit, the follow-up,

Anyone Who Had a Heart, placed the strings a bit further back in the mix and showcased Warwick's voice.

As close to pure pop as much of Warwick's best work is, her vocals never stray too far from the gospel path. Possibly her best record, 1964's **Walk on By**, was a masterpiece of churchy phrasing and subtle melisma that transcended the god-awful horn line. As the Beatles were conquering America, Warwick continued to hit the charts with letter-perfect, controlled performances on songs like **Reach Out For Me** and **You'll Never Get to Heaven (If You Break My Heart)**. Probably because she worked with the kings of middle-class respectability, Warwick hardly raised her voice after "Don't Make Me Over" and, rather like Nat "King" Cole, chose to contain her pain beneath the surface, masking it with extreme stylisation.

No one since Cole himself was as good an interpreter of classic pop material as Warwick. Her soul mannerisms gave warmth to Bacharach's often acerbic arrangements and a gravity to David's trifles like **Trains and Boats and Planes**. Aside from her theme to *Valley of the Dolls*, Warwick's biggest hit of the '60s was **I Say a Little Prayer**, which epitomised her approach to Brill Building product. Although the gospelese call-and-response of "Walk on By" was replaced by bubble-machine "ba-ba-ba-bas" and "oo-oo-oos", Warwick modulated subtly between the church and the cabaret, and "I Say a Little Prayer" was nearly as great a co-mingling of chitlin-circuit grits and showbiz glitz.

Warwick's records with Bacharach-David were unprecedented, yet she didn't have a #1 single until after Bacharach and David broke up. Her 1974 hit with The Spinners, "Then Came You" (not included here), was fine AM radio fodder, but it was hardly her best record. Unfortunately, her career only sank to more pathetic lows with "Heartbreaker" (with Barry Gibb) and "That's What Friends Are For" (with Elton John, Gladys Knight and Stevie Wonder) becoming some of the biggest hits of her career. Then, there was *Solid Gold. . .*

⊃ We almost chose **Hidden Gems**, Rhino, 1992

84

Jackie Wilson

The Very Best of Jackie Wilson

Ace, 1987

Although Jackie Wilson's records are not among the cream of the crop, it's not hard to see why many soul aficionados consider Wilson to be the finest singer of 'em all. Burdened with arrangements that trawled the depths of Mitch Miller/Frank Chacksfield/Floyd Cramer easy-listening territory, Wilson managed to excavate credible records from the most irredeemable schlock by virtue of a remarkable voice. Even though at his very worst (check out Night – an arrangement so archaic it would've sounded square to Lawrence Welk) Wilson sublimated his stunning melisma to the scriptures of inept producers, Wilson always stamped his records with the authority of a consummate performer.

Wilson's peerless showmanship was the product of years spent at the altar of Clyde McPhatter. Not only was McPhatter one of the first secular singers to incorporate gospel phrasing, he was also probably the first to incorporate its physicality into his act. McPhatter would shake, shimmy, glide, stride and drop to his knees while performing and his enactment of ecstasy would create one of black showbiz's most enduring tropes. Wilson studied McPhatter so much that the moves became his own, and after being spotted at a Detroit talent show he became the natural replacement for McPhatter when he left the Dominoes.

Wilson sang with the Dominoes for three years before going solo in 1957. Wilson met up with his cousin Billy Davis, who was writing songs (under the pseudonym Tyrone Carlo) with a failed record store owner called Berry Gordy, and they persuaded

Wilson to record their composition, Reet Petite. Aside from starting the ball rolling for Gordy, "Reet Petite" also set the pattern that would plague Wilson for most of his career. Gordy was a jazz fan who turned to writing pop only when his jazz record store closed down and the lyrics to (not to mention arrangement of) "Reet Petite" were only as hip as a ten-year-old Louis Jordan record by almost the same name. Nonetheless, with his tongue rolls, stylised moans and sudden falsetto leaps, Wilson overcame it all to create a great record.

Gordy and Davis would continue to write hits for Wilson for the next couple of years – To Be Loved, That's Why (I Love You So) and I'll Be Satisfied – the finest of which was Lonely Teardrops. Despite that Swingle Singers chorus, "Lonely Teardrops" featured the best arrangement Wilson would be graced with until 1967 and Wilson gave what may be the best performance of his career. After Gordy left the partnership to start a little record company called Motown, Wilson would continue to enjoy hits until 1963, when no one could forgive the overwrought accompaniments any more. 1960's Doggin' Around could've been off Ray Charles's C&W album from the next year, but Wilson's vocal is again shattering, the sound of a man crying his guts out.

After 1963's Baby Workout, which Wilson actually makes sound as swinging as it wants to be (but just listen to how clumsy the music really is), he wouldn't have another hit until 1966. Finally working with a competent producer (Carl Davis), Wilson had material worthy of his talent on tracks like Whispers and I Get the Sweetest Feeling. Even on these records, however, Davis's Chicago soul style was a bit sickly. The one record where Wilson's voice and music are in harmony was 1967's (Your Love Keeps Lifting Me) Higher and Higher. With a rhythm section that actually drives, a female chorus that had heard of a blue note, tasteful strings and horns that knew that the Bar-Kays wasn't a brand of margarine, Wilson sings like he's found heaven.

⟳We almost chose **The Jackie Wilson Story**, Epic, 1983

85

Womack & Womack

Love Wars

Elektra, 1983

Possibly the most talented family in soul history, the Womacks have been making rock-solid R&B in one form or another since the late 1950s. The Womacks started out as a gospel-singing brother act before they changed their name to the Valentinos in the early '60s and signed to Sam Cooke's SAR label. After recording classics like "It's All Over Now" and "Lookin' For a Love", the group broke up and Bobby Womack went on to have an illustrious career as a solo performer, songwriter and sideman (he played on such epochal records as Sly & the Family Stone's "Family Affair", Wilson Pickett's "Funky Broadway" and Aretha Franklin's first recordings for Atlantic). Bobby's brother, Cecil, meanwhile became a journeyman producer and songwriter, working most notably with his first wife, Mary Wells, on her late '60s/early '70s recordings.

After divorcing Wells, Cecil married Sam Cooke's daughter, Linda, started a songwriting partnership (most notably "Love T.K.O.", which was a big hit for Teddy Pendergrass) and formed Womack & Womack with her in the early '80s. Their first album, **Love Wars**, is a rapprochement of age-old Southern soul verities with new-fangled production values. Musically, it's reminiscent of an Al Green album, but with the Hi Rhythm Section replaced by Linn drums, Fender Rhodes and Ensoniq Mirages and wrapped up in the kind of production sheen that became the hallmark of Philadelphia International during its last days under Dexter Wansel. *Love Wars* also recognises that there's a world of sound outside of Memphis, and Brazilian percussion master Paulinho Da Costa guests on a couple of tracks, while drummer James Gadson was surely listening to Guadeloupe's zouk kingpins Kassav' before coming up with his beat on Baby, I'm Scared of You.

While the music doesn't have the mytho-poetic force of great country soul, the smooth contours and easy lines channel your attention to the words which refine Southern soul's earthy metaphors for urban sophisticates. The resulting songs are among the finest duets since Marvin Gaye and Tammi Terrell. Love Wars ain't no cozy, lovey-dovey, private husband-and-wife thing, though. This is much closer to the brutal metaphors and bitter recriminations of Richard and Linda Thompson's "Shoot Out the Lights" than to the domestic bliss of a Paul and Linda McCartney album. The album's opening number is a synth-bass-driven gospel hymn to peace with an estranged lover begging his partner to "drop them guns on the floor", which leads in to Express Myself – a discourse on love's pleasure/pain dynamic. They put a little gloss on the Rolling Stones' haggard, end-of-the-road ballad, Angie, and do their own version of "Love T.K.O." (called T.K.O. here) which, although not as good as Pendergrass's version (Cecil isn't as good a singer), is plenty ravaged and washed out. Elsewhere, a wife goes AWOL and spends the cuckold's money "like a movie star", lovers are enemies and a woman refuses to be the hunter's trophy.

Throughout the record she is always hip to his sweet-talking and knows better. On Catch and Don't Look Back, his "rap is kind of smooth, but [she] ain't gonna play [his] fool". On Love Wars' masterpiece, "Baby I'm Scared of You", she warns against Houdinis and their tricks. Over a surging, lite-funk background that made the track a big American club hit, the two Womacks create the best wooing dialogue-cum-cautionary tale since Mickey & Sylvia's "Love Is Strange". Unlike "Love Is Strange", though, on "Baby I'm Scared of You" she never calls her lover boy and leaves her suitor to pull rabbits out of his hat for someone else.

⮑ We almost chose **Conscience**, Island, 1988

86

Stevie Wonder

Innervisions

Motown, 1973

Born in 1950, Steveland Morris was a pop star by the time he was 13 years old. The harmonica (mostly) instrumental "Fingertips (Part 2)" might have seemed like a gimmick when it hit #1 in 1963, but the renamed Stevie Wonder never became a washed-up and bitter child star because of a talent that extended well beyond flashy harp runs and youthful energy. Over the next seven years, Wonder released a string of superb singles, like "Uptight (Everything's Alright)", "I Was Made to Love Her", "Heaven Help Us All" and "Signed, Sealed, Delivered, I'm Yours", co-wrote "The Tears of a Clown" with Smokey Robinson and produced the Spinners' "It's a Shame".

In 1971 Wonder's contract with Motown was up for renewal and he demanded complete control over his projects. Like Marvin Gaye, who wanted similar terms, he eventually won, but not without a scrap. Motown had spent all of its history papering over the cracks of racial strife, creating a fantasy world where blacks and whites listened, danced, made out and broke up to the same music. When Gaye and Wonder demanded creative control of their records, they wanted to articulate a vision that was light years away from Berry Gordy's crossover Eden of deportment lessons, proper diction and smiling faces. In the face of race riots, Civil Rights legislation falling short of its promises, and the innovations of Sly Stone, Wonder wanted to sing, "This place is cruel, nowhere could be much colder/If we don't change, the world will soon be over".

Still only 23 when it was released, **Innervisions** was Wonder's most fully realised, most political and best album. Recorded with synthesists Robert Margouleff and Malcolm Cecil (later to become Tonto's Expanding Head Band), *Innervisions* incorporated the resolutely unearthly sounds of the Moog into a sound-world that explicitly engaged with the here and now. The album sought solace from the betrayals and lies of politics, drugs and false religion that plagued black America at the time, but unlike artists like Parliament-Funkadelic and Dexter Wansel, who would use the Moog mostly to imagine a better world far away from earth, Wonder used the Moog mostly to give instrumental voice to the backstabbers, double-crossers and money men from whom he was trying to escape.

As he did with the previous year's "Superstition", Wonder created a tough, buzzing Moog riff that seemed to mirror the chaos he was singing about for one of the album's highlights, Higher Ground. One of *Innervision*'s obsessions is false religion and, even here, a song about reaching heaven, the track fades out before the final lines according to the lyric sheet, "God is gonna show you higher ground/He's the only friend you have around". The equally great Jesus Children of America follows with a similar riff and lyrics that chastise Holy Rollers, transcendental meditationists and junkies. Even the album's centrepiece, the very worldly Living for the City (called the greatest hip-hop skit of all time by producer Prince Paul), was constructed around a churchy organ line and conceived as a quasi-biblical parable. With such a tone, the "smiling faces" trope of '70s soul unsurprisingly rears its head on both Don't You Worry About a Thing and He's Misstra Know-it-All.

While everybody always notes that Wonder turned soul into a genre capable of album-length statements, perhaps his most important innovation of the early '70s was that he collapsed the two oppositions of the male African-American vocal tradition – the fragile, feminised falsetto and the assertive, growling tenor – into each other, creating a persona that was as complex and multi-layered as anyone in pop music, black or white.

⊃We almost chose **Talking Book**, Motown, 1972

87

Various Artists

Badmutha's

Music Collection International, 1998

It's not perfect, but, warts and all, **Badmutha's** is one of the best available overviews of the blaxploitation soundtracks that dominated the soul music of the early to mid-1970s. Just as blaxploitation films were a reaction against the letter-perfect morality of the roles given to Sidney Poitier, the musicians composing the music for films like *Slaughter!*, *Black Gestapo* and Black Shampoo were reacting against the mannered leitmotifs and cod-jazz of Quincy Jones' soundtracks to Poitier films like *In the Heat of the Night* and *They Call Me Mister Tibbs!* With Norman Whitfield's sweeping productions for the Temptations and the Undisputed Truth as a starting point, musicians as diverse as Isaac Hayes, Curtis Mayfield, Roy Ayers, Earth, Wind & Fire and War tried to work the funk, effects pedals, social commentary and a bit of ghetto fabulousness into the standard formulas of soundtrack construction, which at that time were as stiff as a grey flannel suit.

Unfortunately, the recent cult of the '70s black action film tends to reduce the genre to a series of outrageous Afros, leather pimp coats and wah-wah licks, thorny fantasies of the black super-stud, cathartic scenes of the Man getting what's coming to him and, maybe if you're lucky, a celebration of Tamara Dobson and Pam Grier kicking serious ass. While there may well be some pleasure to be had watching a neon-violet, velour jumpsuit strut across the screen, such superfly fetishism reduces the potency of the black style politics of the '70s to nothing but content-free image.

The assertive camouflaging of grim inner-city realities by ridiculously wide lapels and enormous hoop earrings had its parallel in songs like the Four Tops' **Are You Man Enough** (from the *Shaft in Africa* soundtrack and included here). With its contribution to the "smiling faces sometimes tell lies" trope of '70s soul ("Can't turn your back on a smiling face"), "Are You Man Enough" is at once a bitter jibe at the ghetto's growing junkie culture and the failure of the Black Power movement, a cautionary tale against the happy-faced lies of the white establishment and a warning that there was something lurking underneath the grotesque smiles of the pickaninny caricature from the deep South. Meanwhile, unapologetic reality tales like Bobby Womack's **Across 110th Street** offered a different slant on political protest and set much of the agenda for the *musique vérité* style of hip-hop.

Although a proto-Earth, Wind & Fire and Melvin Van Peebles were the first blaxploiters with their psychedelic, Ramsey Lewis-esque score for *Sweet Sweetback's Baadasss Song – ¡Sabroso!* (the title track is included here), it is the wah-wah riff of the gods from Isaac Hayes' (with some help from the Bar-Kays) **Theme from Shaft** that will forever be associated with the genre and it's surprising that for a "definitive" compilation there are no epic chase/fight themes included, like "Pursuit of the Pimp Mobile" from Isaac Hayes' *Truck Turner* soundtrack or "Brawling Broads" from Roy Ayers' *Coffy* soundtrack. *Badmutha's* also lacks any of the painfully oily, love-scene quiet storms, which always had titles like "Buns o' Plenty", "Cleo's Apartment" or "Coffy Sauna" – not that you necessarily need to hear 'em; just they would have given a fuller picture.

These are small complaints, though, and any compilation hip enough to have Willie Hutch practically inventing disco on **Theme From The Mack**, the Blackbyrds' fat, funky and fresh title track from **Cornbread**, Joe Simon's 21-vocal-cord salute to **Cleopatra Jones** and Don Julian's band vamping to the death on **Theme From Savage!** is worth its weight in Afro Sheen.

⮌We almost chose **The Big Score**, EMI, 1998

88

Various Artists

Birth of Soul Volume Two

Kent, 1998

Soul's standard creation myth usually goes something like this: with his gospel style and worldly concerns, Ray Charles brought Saturday night and Sunday morning crashing together in a furious blast of heat, energy, physicality and emotion that would eventually be called soul music. There was no big bang, but a steady progression of different influences coalescing into something just about unified enough to be categorised under one heading. Of course, with antecedents as diverse as gospel, girl groups, doo-wop, Brill Building pop and the blues, and end products as dissimilar as Motown, Stax, Uptown soul and Chicago soul, soul music is difficult to get a handle on. Reminding us what a slippery beast soul is, British soul aficionados Trevor Churchill, Adrian Croasdell and Dave Godin have put together the *Birth of Soul* series, not to provide a definitive prehistory of soul, but to highlight the various strands of music that came together under that banner. Of the two volumes released so far, **Birth of Soul Volume Two** gets the edge because its mix of obscurities and bona fide classics is just right.

If *Birth of Soul Volume Two* slips up, it's because it plays its trump cards first. The Caravans' utterly sublime Walk Around Heaven All Day leads off the compilation. Founded by Albertina Walker, the Caravans were one of the greatest gospel groups of all time, featuring singers like Bessie Griffin, Inez Andrews and Cassietta George. On "Walk Around Heaven" the soloist is the great Shirley Caesar, who gives a masterclass on phrasing, colouring, pacing and control. From the same year (1964), the Invincibles move falsetto singing and extreme devotion out of the church on **Heart Full of Love**. It may be secular, but it would be impossible to call this gorgeous record profane.

Gene Chandler's **Man's Temptation** is equally glorious and stands as a letter-perfect exposition of the virtues of Chicago soul – sweet harmonies, understated vocals, laid-back tempo and a Rousseau-esque fantasy jungle of sound. The Diplomats follow with **Here's a Heart**, which is like a mature doo-wop track – a chorus that runs an octave lower than normal and an intense, gritty lead vocal closer to the pulpit than the street corner. The Drifters' landmark **There Goes My Baby** follows with Ben E. King's abject vocals and over-the-top orchestration combining to create a record that could only ever have been concocted in the heads of producers Jerry Leiber and Mike Stoller rather than in the church or on the streets.

Just as Motown was beginning to develop the "sound of young America", Marie Knight, a 37-year-old singer, was combining Tin Pan Alley, lovelorn-teen lyrics with an explicitly adult, almost operatic, vocal style. Knight's almost archaic style made analysing soul's constituent elements something only fools did at their peril. A year later, in 1962, the Falcons, featuring Wilson Pickett on the remarkable **I Found a Love**, howled at the moon like the Five Blind Boys of Mississippi's Archie Brownlee shouted at the devil. Not even James Brown would ever sound as primal as Pickett does here.

Elsewhere on this superb collection, there's Ray Charles turning gospel's call-and-response technique into swinging audio porn; the Showmen's General Johnson conjuring as many strange and wonderful sounds from his throat as any scat singer; Benny Spellman and Willie Tee singing in a Nworlins drawl lazier than gooey molasses; Solomon Burke giving Otis Redding a few ideas on **Down in the Valley**; the Wallace Brother's miles-deep **Lover's Prayer**; the rough-and-ready harmonies of the unjustly obscure Eddie & Ernie, and Vernell Hill's outrageous combination of Julie London and the Shirelles on **Long Haired Daddy**.

⮎We almost chose **Birth of Soul Volume One**, Kent, 1996

89

Various Artists

Kurtis Blow Presents the History of Rap Vol. 1

Rhino, 1997

Moving chronologically from 1970 to 1979, **Kurtis Blow Presents The History of Rap Vol. 1** maps the death of what had become known as soul music. Soul, particularly Southern soul, had developed in tandem with the Civil Rights movement, a struggle with a defined goal and distinct ambitions. However, Civil Rights legislation largely failed to address the grievances of the urban ghettos, which, despite the efforts of groups like the Black Panthers and the Black Arts movement, were never articulated into a coherent programme for change. Anything but a narrative about crossing over the River Jordan into the promised land, hip-hop was the music that grew out of the abandonment of the Northern inner cities. A profound statement of dislocation and alienation, hip-hop was pieced together out of the ready-mades found in the cultural scrapheap of capitalism's capital city. Collaging five-second passages of obscure and not-so-obscure records, hip-hop's architects jerry-built a Rube Goldberg contraption that spoke to post-Civil Rights kids and redefined the musical landscape. *The History of Rap Vol. 1* collects the base material that hip-hop's scavenger-alchemists eventually turned into gold and platinum.

Hip-hop was first ignited when Kool DJ Herc tapped into the New York City power supply at a Bronx block party in the early '70s. Herc was a Jamaican DJ who had emigrated to the US in 1967 and set up his own sound system in the Bronx. When his reggae records failed to move the crowd, he turned to funk, but the only part of the records he would play was the short section where all the instrumentalists dropped out except for the percussionists. The "break" was the part of the record that the dancers wanted to hear anyway, so he isolated it by playing two copies of the same record on two turntables – when the break on one turntable finished, he would play it on the other turntable. Herc's breakbeat style of DJing was much in demand and soon other DJs like Grandmaster Flash, Afrika Bambaataa and Grand Wizard Theodore emerged playing a similar style of music, but with greater skill and more technological sophistication.

The breakbeat was hip-hop's DNA and the breaks of the records collected here were early classics at block parties and clubs like The Disco Fever. Although it was the DJs themselves who articulated hip-hop's shock of the new, the records they used followed a new rhythmic impetus that had started with James Brown and Dyke & the Blazers. This wasn't just funk – bands like the Ohio Players or Cameo didn't have much in the way of breaks and P-Funk didn't get a look in until hip-hop had migrated to the left coast – the DJs were after a kind of low-end militancy and the records they chose were full of drum tattoos, black holes of bass, scorched-earth screams and searing guitars. Check Jimmy Castor's It's Just Begun – a roiling bass-line and insistent flanged guitars build a manic intensity brought to boiling point by the Latin percussion and scything guitar solo of the break – or the greatest break of 'em all and the b-boys' (break boys, the dancers) national anthem, the Incredible Bongo Band's Apache, which sounded like a drum phalanx marching on the bandits in a spaghetti western flick for the best examples of this aesthetic. It's not just coincidence that most of these titles are imperatives (Get into Something, Listen to Me, Give It Up or Turnit a Loose) or filled with warlike images ("Apache", Theme from S.W.A.T.) – unlike soul, hip-hop wasn't turning the other cheek; it was staking a claim and asserting itself.

⮑We almost chose **DJ Pogo Presents Block Party Breaks**, Strut, 1999

90

Various Artists

Classic Salsoul Mastercuts Volume 1

Mastercuts, 1993

Disco will always be pooh-poohed by purists who insist that music must aspire to something beneath its surface and deny that art is part of artifice. These are often the same people who think that real soul music was unsullied by commerce and made in a racial vacuum. But while fundamentalists devote themselves to their Percy Sledges and Solomon Burkes, hedonists and heretics will gladly defile themselves in the rhinestone glamour, garish synth colours and strictly funktional rhythms of the beat that never stopped.

Salsoul was the best disco label there was. Founded in 1973 as Mericana Records by the Cayre brothers, Salsoul began as a company specialising in Latin music. Amongst its albums by Grupo Folklorico y Experimental Nuevayorquino and Saoco, Mericana released an album by Afro-Filipino pianist and vocalist Joe Bataan called *Salsoul* in 1973. The streamlined combination of salsa and soul on cuts like "Latin Strut" and "Aftershower Funk" became favourites in New York clubs and Mericana was soon renamed in honour of its biggest record. Bataan's follow-up album, *Afro-Filipino*, released the following year, included "La Botella", a version of Gil Scott-Heron's "The Bottle". Further refining the combination of salsa and soul, "La Botella" had percolating montuno-derived rhythms and piano passages underneath distinctly midtown horns courtesy of David Sanborn. You can argue that the Temptations' "Law of the Land" or Patti Jo's "Make Me Believe in You" were the first disco records, but as a specific genre, rather than an aesthetic, disco started right here.

Although created in New York, much of disco's sound was based on the "Sound of Philadelphia". The lush orchestrations and upwardly mobile funk of Philadelphia International's house band, MFSB, laid the foundations. Following the model of MFSB, Salsoul created their own house band, the Salsoul Orchestra, led by vibist Vince Montana Jr. In addition to their own records, they would play on the large majority of the label's output, backing everyone from Loleatta Holloway to Charo.

Following the Gamble and Huff formula to the letter, the Salsoul Orchestra was behind Double Exposure for the all-time classic, Ten Percent. The production of MFSB/SOers Ronnie Baker, Norman Harris and Earl Young was devastating, but "Ten Percent" will go down in history because it was the first commercially available 12" single. Mixed by the legendary Walter Gibbons, "Ten Percent" became a nine-minute epic with boosted ride cymbals (a sound which has dominated dance music for twenty years) and extended, chopped, looped instrumental passages.

As luck would have it, the only two challengers to Gibbons' title as the greatest remixer of them all contributed themselves to Salsoul's dance-floor pre-eminence. The patron saint of disco, Larry Levan, turned in one of the most implausible remixes ever in the shape of his keyboard-odyssey/soft-porn-vignette rework of Instant Funk's I Got My Mind Up. Meanwhile, years before he worked with Madonna, Shep Pettibone crafted Salsoul's two greatest records. First Choice's Let No Man Put Asunder from 1977 is not only one of the ten or fifteen most sampled records, but, more importantly, it basically created the blueprint for house music. Three years later, as disco as a mainstream phenomenon was dying, Pettibone, producer/songwriter Dan Hartman and vocalist Loleatta Holloway delivered a love letter to the disco underground with perhaps the ultimate disco record, Love Sensation. And, if you don't think that Holloway's exorcism of pain merits a place in the soul continuum, you deserve all those Jon Lucien and Terry Callier records you probably listen to.

⮑We almost chose **Classic Salsoul**
Mastercuts Volume 2, Mastercuts, 1993

91

Various Artists

Keb Darge's Legendary Deep Funk Volume 1

Barely Breaking Even, 1997

Record collectors are a strange lot. Stories abound of people who have facsimile collections at different locations in case something should happen to their precious booty, or there's the guy in New York who goes into the Tower Records sale annex every two hours to check if they've put out anything new. Keb Darge is no different: he's part of that cabal of celebrity collectors (Russ Dewbury, Gilles Peterson, Norman Jay) who are responsible for the UK's Northern soul/rare groove/jazz-funk celebrations of African-American musical arcana by virtue of their willingness to shimmy up drainpipes to get into boarded-up record warehouses in Harlem to rescue impossibly obscure records from the hungry mouths of rabid rats. What separates Darge from his contemporaries, however, is his taste, and what separates his *Legendary Deep Funk* series from the deluge of dodgy rare-funk bootlegs is that it's legal and the label tries to pay royalties to the artists.

Darge is a Scottish veteran of the Northern soul scene with notoriously uncompromising views on music and fashion victims. While his hectoring of party poopers and pissheads during his DJ sets doesn't do much to endear him to non-die-hards, his passion translates to his curatorial skills and wins him friends in the murky world of rare record dealers who cater to his funk passion. This first volume of his *Legendary Deep Funk* series comes with the impressive tag that the sum cost of the loot collected here would be £5000 if bought individually. But does £5000 necessarily buy more quality than £12.99 plucked down at HMV on a decent James Brown reissue?

The answer, of course, is probably no, but that doesn't mean that this isn't an essential album, especially since you don't have to pay £5000 for it. **Keb Darge's Legendary Deep Funk Volume 1** begins with a ferocious organ and wah-wah instrumental called Zambezi by the Fun Company, which neatly sums up the kind of music championed by Darge. With its wailing Hammond clarion call in the intro and the bubbling, strutting bass-line, "Zambezi" is a blistering, hard funk tune that evokes images of a tiny, run-down Southern studio run by chancers hoping to become the next Stax. "Zambezi" is followed by Ernie & the Topnotes' legendary Dap Walk, which may be a rip-off of Archie Bell & the Drells but has so much vim and vigour that it's hard to be a spoil-sport.

The best of the remaining tracks on *Legendary Deep Funk Volume 1* are similarly styled '60s cuts like Big Bo Thomas and the Arrows' Mar-Keys-esque How About It. The shuffling rhythm and Sam Butera sax of the Originals Orchestra's version of Monk Higgins' Who Dun It is simply irresistible, while Lil Ray and the Fantastic Four's Soul Power sounds like a combination between b-boy favourites S.O.U.L. and the Mohawks. By the time the '70s hit, the fidelity of better quality and the chirpy weirdness subsided, to be replaced by a lame jazziness. There are a few gems from this period here, though. Cross Bronx Expressway's eponymous offering moves in a way that the New York road it's named after never does, while Smokin' Shades of Black's Grease Wheels sounds like it's rolling down Eddie Palmieri's Harlem River Drive with its salsa-fied horn-line and timbale break.

As on any funk reissue, there is some dross on offer, to be sure (rarity is certainly no guarantee of quality). But how often do you hear a record these days called The (Rockin') Courtroom or a group calling themselves Judge Suds and the Soul Detergents?

⮑ We almost chose **Keb Darge's Legendary Deep Funk Volumes 2 and 3**, Barely Breaking Even, 1998, 1999

92

Various Artists

Freestyle's Greatest Beats: The Complete Collection Volume 1

Tommy Boy/Timber, 1994

None of pop's miscegenated couplings has been more bizarre than kids from the Bronx believing that Düsseldorf's showroom dummies Kraftwerk were the funkiest thing since James Brown. Borrowing heavily from Kraftwerk's "Trans-Europe Express" and "Numbers", Afrika Bambaataa & the Soul Sonic Force's "Planet Rock" introduced the video-game aesthetic that dominated New York's dance music scene during the 1980s. With the increasing availability of fairly sophisticated technology, the sound of harsh drum machines and piercing synthesizers on records like C-Bank's "One More Shot" and Planet Patrol's "Play At Your Own Risk" defined Gotham's clubscape in the early '80s. Somewhere in this mechanical matrix, New York Latinos heard ancestral echoes of salsa piano lines and montuno rhythms. In the hands of producers like the Latin Rascals, Paul Robb, Omar Santana and Andy "Panda" Tripoli, the Pac-Man bleeps, synth stabs and Roland TR-808 clavés became an android descarga called Freestyle.

Freestyle was the kind of thing that could only happen in New York and, with the exception of Miami and its large Hispanic community, it was largely ignored by the rest of the nation. Make no mistake, though: Freestyle exerted an enormous influence on dance music producers and, with the exception of the brief flourishes of East Side soul in LA and Latin Rock, it was the first mainstream genre that Hispanic Americans could call their own. **Freestyle's**

Greatest Beats: The Complete Collection Volume 1 contains most of the major recordings from Freestyle's golden age in the mid-'80s and is probably the single best collection available.

Freestyle's ground zero was Shannon's 1983 single, "Let the Music Play". Although it didn't have the hi-hat sound that would come to characterise Freestyle percussion, the track's electro-wood-block-and-cowbell percussion and kick drum/snare drum interaction provided the blueprint for Freestyle's street-smart tales of innocence and experience. **Please Don't Go** (1984), by 16-year-old Nayobe and produced by Andy Panda, further Latinised the formula by featuring keyboard patterns stolen from Eddie Palmieri and Patrice Rushen on top of synthesised timbale beats. Also in 1984, Funhouse DJ Jellybean Benitez attempted to reclaim **The Mexican** for Latinos from both Ennio Morricone and prog rock group Babe Ruth.

Former Funhouse dancer Lisa Velez was discovered by production team Full Force and, as Lisa Lisa, became Freestyle's biggest early star. With a dubby synth effect stolen from John Robie's Emulator keyboard and a Roland wood-block pattern, Lisa Lisa & Cult Jam's debut record, **I Wonder If I Take You Home** (1984) dented the American Top 40 when it was re-released by Columbia in 1985. Other early stars included the proto-boy-band trio TKA and "the Latin Supremes" the Cover Girls, whose **One Way Love** and **Show Me** are included here.

Largely adenoidal teenagers, most of Freestyle's vocalists could barely hold a note without their voices cracking, let alone compete with the singers of the soul tradition. If, as its many guardians claim, however, soul music is about the direct expression of experience, then Freestyle, with its emphasis on heartbreak vocals and stirring melody, surely deserves a place in its pantheon. That Freestyle transcends its largely crass teenybop foundations is down to the producers and mixers who not only created startling electronic music, but made their knob-twiddling signify as the musical analogue of vocalists grasping for certainty amid change and flux.

⮑ We almost chose **Freestyle's Greatest Beats Volume 2**, Tommy Boy/Timber, 1994

93

Various Artists

Dave Godin's Deep Soul Treasures Volume 1

Kent, 1997

The trouble with British soul obsessives is that they often willingly sacrifice quality in favour of rarity and obscurity. Dave Godin, however, is a limey R&B archivist you can trust. As a proselytising columnist for *Blues & Soul* magazine during the 1960s and '70s, and as the head of the Deep Soul and Soul City labels, Godin was directly responsible for weaning people off Cilla Black and Lulu covers in favour of the genuine article. More importantly, the original soul evangelist was responsible for encouraging Motown to release their records in the UK. So, when he describes something as "deep", you can be sure it doesn't refer to the record's position in the dusty, dark unknown of his collection.

In recent years, "deep" has become a word to fear when it is used to describe music. The talisman for dance music's guardians of taste and "propriety" who are really only guarding their own slice of the entrepreneurial pie, "depth" has come to signify vaguely jazzy chords, relaxed tempos and late-night ambience. For Godin, however, "Deep Soul is never mellow, and it is never bland . . . In point of fact, Deep Soul sets its face firmly against such emotional compromises . . . " The records that Godin compiles for this series are, with one or two exceptions, all about break-up catharsis and pull no punches when it comes to emotional expression. Listen to something like Sam & Bill's "I Feel Like Cryin'" from **Dave Godin's Deep Soul Treasures Volume 1** and it is immediately apparent that this collection has absolutely nothing to do with watery keyboard colours and spurious notions of jazz and everything to do with gritty blue notes and soaring gospel melisma.

The drunken Memphis horns and bittersweet testifying of I Feel Like Cryin' highlights the singular triumph of the *Deep Soul Treasures* series: almost every one of these obscurities should be talked of in the same exalted tones normally reserved for Otis Redding, Sam Cooke and Aretha Franklin. The Knight Brothers' I'm Never Gonna Live it Down is a huge, overwhelming track full of cascading drums, vocals that just about manage not to drown in the instrumental whirlpool, guitar chanks and roiling horns that is the pinnacle of Chicago soul. The peerless melodrama of Anyone Who Knows What Love Is (Will Understand) (a song co-written by Randy Newman) by the criminally underappreciated Irma Thomas proves that it wasn't just Ray Charles who could make countrypolitan chorales signify like a sanctified church choir. Even an artist like Dori Grayson – someone so obscure that Godin himself had no idea who she was – creates a broken-hearted plea that exorcises romantic demons with the best of them.

Deep Soul Treasures Volume 1 also features Timmy Willis scandalously ripping off Otis Redding to great effect, galloping urgency and string sweetening from Barry White on Brendetta Davis's (aka Brenda Holloway) I Can't Make it Without Him, ebbing and flowing regret from Larry Banks and Raw Spitt's stunning protest song, Songs to Sing. The highlight, however, is Jean Wells' Have a Little Mercy – one of those beautiful tracks where the vocalist's barely contained restraint and the slowly building rhythm section say more than any number of whoops, hollers and mannered shouts ever could.

Elsewhere on *Deep Soul Treasures Volume 1* such truly underground artists as Kenny Carter, Jimmy Holiday, the Incredibles and Van & Titus all wreck the house and make convincing arguments that perhaps soul's canon should be as big as the Brits think it should.

⤴ We almost chose **Deep Soul Treasures Volume 2**, Kent, 1999

94

Various Artists

The Great Gospel Women Vol. 2

Shanachie, 1995

It's hardly surprising that, aside from womyn's music of course, gospel is the genre that is most dominated by female singers. Religion has always been considered a "woman's concern" and in the church women have been allowed to develop as singers largely protected from the male prejudices and vampirism that haunt the less salubrious corners of the music industry. With the notable exceptions of Sam Cooke and Al Green, male soul singers have pledged their undying devotion to love and sex and left the church behind. For female soul singers, on the other hand, the distinctions between the secular and the sacred are more blurred. Thus, they have greater ties to the gospel tradition, and the music collected here is both closer to, and in some ways farther away from, soul than that of their male counterparts. Compiled by leading gospel historian Anthony Heilbut, both volumes of **The Great Gospel Women** contain stunning music, but **Volume 2** gets the slight edge because it concentrates less on Mahalia Jackson and Marion Williams and spreads the joy amongst seventeen singers both famous and obscure.

The album leads off with four cuts from Mahalia Jackson, and suffice it to say that the performances included here are staggering. Probably the most famous gospel singer after Jackson was Sister Rosetta Tharpe. Tharpe was raised in the Pentecostal Church and was the bluesiest of all the female gospel singers. One of her numbers here, That's All, was originally titled "Denomination Blues" and, change a word here and there, could have been heard at any roadhouse in the South during the 1930s and '40s. Tharpe's expressive voice quickly made her the most commercially successful gospel artist of the day and her influence and esteem was such that she was Elvis's favourite gospel singer.

Along with Jackson and Tharpe, Clara Ward is considered the greatest female gospel singer. With her slightly nasal voice, slurred notes and potent vibrato, Ward was an individualistic stylist. She teamed up with Reverend C.L. Franklin in the '50s and the debt his daughter Aretha owes to her is obvious, particularly on Ward's phrasing of Heaven My Home. The Ward Singers were the most influential group of the '40s and '50s, introducing soloists like Frances Steadman and Marion Williams. More than one critic has called Williams the greatest singer ever, and it's hard to disagree. Too demonstrative to settle safely into pop's constraints, Williams revelled in the gospel tradition and she exploited this freedom with some of the most amazing flights ever captured on vinyl.

Gospel remains a mystery to most folks outside of the church and one of the glories of *The Great Gospel Women* is its introduction of some of the more peripheral figures. She might not be a household name, but Edna Gallmon Cooke was an absolute master of moaning and melisma, and on both I've Got Religion and Build Me a Cabin you can clearly hear echoes of the house-wrecking style that the more powerful female soul singers would borrow a decade or so later. The same is true of Marie Knight, who used to be Rosetta Tharpe's partner, but has been erased from all but the most complete gospel histories. She may have been belting out of ecstasy on God Spoke to Me, but the shrieking paranoia and lust that would come to characterise the very best soul has its roots right here. That's just the first half of the CD; the rest includes just as vital performances from people like Bessie Griffin, Jesse Mae Renfro and Mary Johnson Davis.

⮑ We almost chose **The Great Gospel Women Volume 1**, Shanachie, 1993

95

Various Artists

Jubilation! Great Gospel Performances Vol. 2

Rhino, 1992

In terms of influence, popularity and endurance, black gospel was the most significant musical form of the twentieth century. Unfortunately, for most gospel practitioners and record buyers, that triumph has been purely formal. Gospel was crystallised as a genre around the same time as jazz and blues, but it has outlived both as a presence on the contemporary music scene. While jazz has become increasingly forced into a tiny ghetto of intellectuals and die-hards, and the blues influence on rock has more or less faded away, the vocal techniques, physicality and intensity of gospel remains the lingua franca of popular music. The music collected on **Jubilation! Great Gospel Performances Vol. 2** is why. Although the first volume of *Jubilation!* is probably the better disc and features music of greater historical importance, *Volume 2* serves the purposes of this book better, and when music is of this quality, second place isn't much of a compromise.

In the popular imagination, gospel is often portrayed as get-happy handclapping music extolling the joys of communion with the Lord. Gospel has its dark side, however, and at its best it's so harrowing it will freeze your blood. Before they went pop, the Staple Singers were one of the most popular groups on the gospel circuit. On their masterpiece, Uncloudy Day, Pops Staples plays a guitar part that is all quaver, shivering like a ghost in the corner, while Mavis's lead vocal and the harmonies echo the chants of the gangs of field hands picking cotton. It was recorded in 1956, but it sounds as ancient and elemental as Mississippi mud. One of the greatest of the gospel shouters, Archie Brownlee of the Five Blind Boys of Mississippi (also called the Jackson Harmoneers) had a bloodcurdling scream that influenced everyone from Screamin' Jay Hawkins to James Brown. Heard here on the chilling Our Father, Brownlee was one of the people responsible for the transition of gospel from the jazzy jubilee style of the '30s to the more emotionally direct style of the Sanctified Church.

Julius Cheeks of the Sensational Nightingales never sang to arrangements as stark as those of the Five Blind Boys of Mississippi, but his voice was even more intense than Brownlee's. Cheeks was Wilson Pickett's direct influence and his unsurpassed intensity can be heard here on the remarkable Burying Ground, perhaps the most powerfully cathartic performance ever caught on vinyl. Its only rival is probably the Swan Silvertones' My Rock, which features the great Paul Owens and Solomon Womack growling with such power that to try to describe it would only serve to trivialise it. Of course, gospel's female singers were just as dynamic and Mahalia Jackson's How I Got Over, the Original Gospel Harmonettes' (You Can't Hurry God) He's Right on Time and the Davis Singers' By and By show you why gospel's physicality became the world's favoured vehicle for expressing worldly ecstasy.

Gospel isn't all brute force and cataclysmic exorcism, however. The Harmonising Four's version of Motherless Child gets over on the perfection of the group's harmonies, while the Soul Stirrers' Jesus, I'll Never Forget showcases the sublime vocals of Sam Cooke. Cooke replaced the legendary R.H. Harris in the Soul Stirrers and his Cooke-like vocals can be heard here on Sell Out to the Master, recorded when he was a member of the Christland Singers. Harris is generally credited with more or less inventing modern harmony-group singing, an innovation which had profound consequences for soul as well as gospel, and this compilation is a testament to his influence.

⮑We almost chose **Jubilation! Great Gospel Performances Vol. 1**, Rhino, 1992

96

Various Artists

Jumpin'

Harmless, 1997

While many commentators of the time thought that the D-word was, as one-hit wonders Ottawan might have put it, "D – distasteful, I – insipid, S – superficial, C – crap, O – *oy vey*", the reality was that disco posed as much of a challenge to the status quo as punk, hip-hop, rock'n'roll or any other "revolutionary" genre of music. Attempting to both banish the veneer of naturalism and authenticity ascribed to black music once and for all and to be the embodiment of the pleasure-is-politics ethos of the emerging Gay Pride movement, disco was a celebration of the fantastic where flash, overwhelming melodrama, sex, surface and fabulousness were all that mattered.

It's true that disco's political thrust may have been largely apprehended only "in the mix". But disco was capable of political statements that even the most die-hard modernist could understand. Take, for instance, Machine's **There But For the Grace of God Go I**. Written and produced by August Darnell (the man responsible for both Dr. Buzzard's Original Savannah Band and Kid Creole & the Coconuts), "There But For the Grace . . ." was a morality play set to a throbbing electro-bass-line, glittering keyboard licks and a four-to-the-floor beat. With dramatic, almost Stephen Sondheim-esque piano chords introducing the action, the song tells the story of Carlo and Carmen Vidale, who move to the suburbs "with no blacks, no Jews and no gays" to raise their kid. With perhaps predictable irony, their daughter eventually turns into a rock'n'roll-loving "natural freak" who runs away from home aged 16. At a time when American inner cities were being ravaged by white flight, the song's message was clear, particularly to a dance floor full of blacks, Jews and gays.

Admittedly, though, "There But For the Grace of God Go I" was a rarity and great songwriting wasn't disco's strong point. Groove was. Disco was at its most revolutionary when it sought to explore new spaces in between the notes. One of disco's great space cadets was Arthur Russell. Russell was one of those peripatetic eccentrics that are seemingly unique to New York. He studied under the great Indian sarod player, Ali Akbar Khan, was a key player in the Big Apple's "new music" scene and collaborated with people like Philip Glass, John Cage and Laurie Anderson. He brought all this to the table when he created his deconstructionist disco. Working with Steve D'Aquisto, Russell created one of the most crucial underground disco cuts, Loose Joints' Is it All Over My Face? Featuring a bass-heavy, but simultaneously airy groove, an almost-out-of-tune guitar, abrupt edits and one of the just plain weirdest vocals ever, "Is it All Over My Face" was completely unique and one of the building blocks of house music. Recording as Dinosaur L, Russell's Go Bang! was even weirder and, in the François Kevorkian mix included here, even more of an influence on subsequent dance music producers.

You didn't have to be a maverick, though, to wander into disco's exploratory space. Jazz-funk jobbers Wood, Brass & Steel (who would eventually mutate into the house band at hip-hop label Sugar Hill) jammed their way into a dubby outer space realm about two minutes into their classic Funkanova. Drum machines are often blamed for disco's rigidity, but one listen to Northend's Tee's Happy and its supremely funky drum-machine calculus should show that lie for the Luddite propaganda that it is.

While there are hundreds of disco compilations with "I Will Survive" and "Got to Be Real" on it, **Jumpin'** is one of the few to feature the underground die-hards and not just the bandwagon-jumpers.

⊃We almost chose **Give Your Body Up: Club Classics and House Foundations Vols. 1–3**, Rhino, 1995

97

Various Artists

Land of 1000 Dances

Ace, 1999

If you're too young to remember any dance crazes earlier than the Hustle or the Electric Slide, then **Land of 1000 Dances** will be a complete eye-opener. In pre-Beatles America just about the only records that mattered were the ones, as they used to say on *American Bandstand*, "that had a good beat you could dance to". This simple maxim applied as much to early soul music as it did to any other form of popular music. Just about all of soul's greatest legends made records that either capitalised on, or started dance crazes: Sam Cooke's "Shake" and "Everybody Loves to Cha Cha Cha", Marvin Gaye's "Hitch Hike" and about half of James Brown's records. Whatever the self-appointed guardians of black music may claim about soaring emotion, true-to-life renderings of heartbreak and "soulfulness", back then even ballads were little more than excuses for slow dances. *Land of 1000 Dances* is perhaps the only collection around that's not ashamed to admit the unrepentantly commercial, unrepentantly novelty origins of the records it collects.

Land of 1000 Dances isn't a pure soul compilation, however. There are ringers from the worlds of rock'n'roll and pop, but most of them don't embarrass themselves in this company: Chan Romero's snarling Hippy Hippy Shake, Tommy James and the Shondells' wonderfully sleazy Hanky Panky, Billy Graves' Carolina beach music classic The Shag (Is Totally Cool), and Bobby "Boris" Pickett's Monster Mash.

It's the soul tracks that make the compilation, however. *Land of 1000 Dances* kicks off with the grandiose horn and timpani intro of Bob & Earl's Harlem Shuffle. Arranged by omnipresent studio hack Gene Page, "Harlem Shuffle" was that rarest of tracks: an orchestral dance record (Earl can also be heard as Jackie Lee on the Motown rip, The Duck). Perhaps even denser was Little Eva's The Loco-Motion. Everything about "The Loco-Motion" seems wrong – the lyrics are overwritten, the arrangement is plodding, Little Eva can't sing – but somehow it all works fantastically to produce an irresistible pop record.

Bert Berns is more well-known as the producer of records by the Drifters, Van Morrison, Solomon Burke, Freddie Scott and Lorraine Ellison, but his two contributions to the dance craze oeuvre are unbeatable. The Isley Brothers' Twist and Shout was produced and written by Berns, while Russell Byrd's Hitch Hike was really a pairing of Bern's kitschy vocals on top of King Curtis's band, producing a definitive document of '60s cool. Another unexpected name to crop up here is Sylvester Stewart, better known as Sly Stone. Before he changed the face of soul music in the late '60s/early '70s, Sly was the in-house producer, arranger and A&R man for San Francisco label Autumn Records. During his tenure there, he wrote and produced Bobby Freeman's intense and swinging C'mon and Swim.

More often than not, however, great dance craze records were created by one-hit wonders. Jimmy McCracklin's super-syncopated The Walk was the sound of a down-on-his-luck blues singer trying his damndest to get a hit single, and succeeding. The Capitols' great Cool Jerk managed to work an honest-to-goodness narrative into their handclapping barnstormer. Before writing Betty Wright's "Clean Up Woman", Steve Alaimo made one of the great blue-eyed soul hits, a wild cover of James Brown's Mashed Potatoes. Including such classics as Johnny Otis's Willie and the Hand Jive, Rufus Thomas's Walking the Dog and Ray Barretto's El Watusi, Land of 1000 Dances is a collection of gloriously simple tracks epitomising pop's basic power that will exorcise the ghosts of Van McCoy and Los Del Rio in no time.

⮌We almost chose **Soul Shots: A Collection of '60s Soul Classics**, Rhino, 1988

98

Various Artists

Larry Levan's Paradise Garage

West End, 1999

In the 1970s the offices of West End Records were just upstairs from Studio 54 on 54th Street in Manhattan. Despite its proximity to the world's most famous disco, most of the label's output was actually aimed at another legendary nightspot two and a half miles away, the Paradise Garage. The Paradise Garage was where the patron saint of dance music, Larry Levan, performed his miracles and it was the home of disco after it had gone back underground in the face of the "Disco Sucks" campaign. Levan was certainly the most influential and inspiring figure on the disco scene and his DJing skills and sensibility are largely responsible for today's mythologising of the DJ. Levan worked closely with the West End label and most of the label's producers, particularly Kenton Nix, worked with him and with his dance floor of mostly gay revellers in mind.

West End was formed by former Scepter executive Mel Cheren in 1976. Cheren was largely responsible for the development of the 12" single and, logically, his label catered to DJs rather than faddists. The label's first release was the title theme to an Italian soft-porn flick, "Sesso Matto" ("Sex Mad"), which would become a hit with both disco hedonists and Bronx b-boys. West End had numerous commercial successes in the '70s, most notably Karen Young's "Hot Shot", but really hit its stride in 1979 with Levan's mix of Billy Nichol's **Give Your Body Up to the Music**. The strain of house known as garage was given its name because it originated at the Paradise Garage and the strange keyboard riffs of "Give Your Body Up ... " show just how house broke away from disco. Crucially, though, West End's best releases stayed close to R&B, and Nichols, a former member of funksters B.T. Express, was a perfect example of this. Of course, the Latin percussion breakdown never let the track stray too far from the rhinestoned groove.

Another crucial 1979 release was Taana Gardner's **Work That Body**. The debut production of Kenton Nix, who would dominate the sound of very early '80s New York with Gardner and Gwen McRae, "Work That Body" had more proto-house keyboards, a killer wah-wah lick, an incredibly liquid bass sound and the skipping hi-hats that would come to define garage.

Gardner's biggest hit, however, was 1981's **Heartbeat**. Featuring one of the most famous bass-lines in the history of dance music (it's been sampled over thirty times by everyone from Ini Kamoze to Snoop Dogg), "Heartbeat" allegedly sold over 100,000 copies in its first week of release in the Big Apple alone. "Heartbeat" was more than just its bass-line and the weird keyboards in the background: the subdued drums and its 98 bpm tempo proved that disco wasn't just the funkless, automaton groove that its detractors claimed.

Almost as popular with today's producers was Loose Joints' **Is It All Over My Face**, produced by the great disco maverick Arthur Russell and Steve D'Aquisto. It was a masterpiece of detached vocals, compressed dynamics and rhythmic minimalism that influenced scores of house producers and remains one of the most unique interpretations of the R&B/soul tradition.

Equally original was **Don't Make Me Wait**, by Levan's own project, the New York Citi Peech Boys. Occupying its own netherworld somewhere between dub and electro, "Don't Make Me Wait" trapped vocalist Bernard Fowler in an echo chamber of spooky sound effects that made his plea for sexual fulfilment sound like it was both foreplay and a curse. It may have sounded like it was made by cyborgs who had never heard of Motown or Stax, but "Don't Make Me Wait" is everything soul music is meant to be, and an enduring monument to Levan (who died in 1992).

⭲We almost chose **The West End Story Volume 2**, West End/Unidisc, 1992

99

Various Artists

The New Orleans Hit Story

Charly, 1997

With a cosmopolitan population that included recent immigrants from the Caribbean, freed slaves and decommissioned soldiers and their marching band instruments, New Orleans at the turn of the twentieth century was the birthplace of modern popular music. From the jazz that developed out of this melting pot to the swinging rhythms of 1950s, '60s and '70s R&B that the original Creole second line beats evolved into, New Orleans has been the epicentre of the most groundbreaking developments of African-American music.

While the Crescent City's marching band heritage has been celebrated elsewhere in this book, its piano players have played just as crucial a role in shaping the direction of soul and R&B. The most famous early New Orleans ivory tinkler was Jelly Roll Morton, who was perhaps the most pivotal figure in the development of jazz (he even claimed to have invented it). Morton's milieu was in the bordellos of the Storyville district, where dozens of piano players developed a syncopated, funky style that was miles away from the European tradition. In the hands of Fats Domino (and his arranger Dave Bartholomew) this Creole style became simultaneously more percussive and more loping. The lazy, easy swing of Fats Domino's records made him one of the biggest pop stars of any era, charting something like 63 singles in the pop charts from 1950 to 1964. Unfortunately he is only represented on **The New Orleans Hit Story** by four live recordings from late in his career, but Domino's piano triplets and his slyly rollicking rhythms (and the even funkier style of Professor

Longhair) are at the root of that undefinable, but instantly recognisable, Nworlins swing.

The other great New Orleans pianist who changed the shape of R&B and soul was Allen Toussaint. As producer/arranger/A&R man/jack of all trades for the Minit label from 1960 until he was drafted in 1963, Toussaint was responsible for the records that made the period between Buddy Holly's death and the emergence of the Beatles better than what preceded it or what came immediately after. Minit's first hit was Jessie Hill's Ooh Poo Pah Doo. Pure Nworlins drawl, "Ooh Poo Pah Doo" combined Mardi Gras Indian chants, rhythmic guitar comping and an insistent horn riff into a swampy bayou of bass that just might be the first funk record. Toussaint followed "Ooh Poo Pah Doo" with a string of equally joyful, equally brilliant records that included Ernie K-Doe's Mother-in-Law and Te-Ta-Te-Ta-Ta (with a horn intro that gave Southern soul its signature sound), Jessie Hill's Whip It On Me, Chris Kenner's I Like It Like That and Land of 1000 Dances, Benny Spellman's Lipstick Traces (On a Cigarette) and Fortune Teller and the Showmen's It Will Stand. Also included here are the hits Toussaint scored with Lee Dorsey and the Meters when he returned to New Orleans from the army in 1965.

By the mid-'60s much of New Orleans' finest talent had emigrated to LA (to work with Phil Spector, among others) and New York. In the Big Apple, Big Easy singer Alvin Robinson hit with the fonkiest record ever to be cut so far away from the bayou, Something You Got, while the Dixie Cups' version of the Mardi Gras chant, Iko Iko, was easily the weirdest record of the girl-group era. Perhaps the most New Orleans artist of all, though, wasn't even from Louisiana. From Macon, Georgia, Little Richard's rock'n'roll records were New Orleans rhythms with his fingers in electrical sockets, but he's represented here by I Don't What You Got (But it's Got Me), a deep soul ballad from 1965 that is one of soul's most undersung recordings.

⮑ We almost chose **Crescent City Soul:**
The Sound of New Orleans, EMI, 1996

100

Various Artists

Prelude's Greatest Hits

Unidisc, 1988

From its foundation in 1977 to its commercial death in 1984, Prelude was second only to Salsoul in its championing of underground New York disco. Providing a home for such dance-music cult heroes as producer Patrick Adams and mixer/DJ extraordinaire François Kevorkian, and giving them the space to experiment, Prelude was probably even more innovative than Salsoul. With labels like Tommy Boy, Streetwise and Sleeping Bag dominating the playlists of the Big Apple's premier radio station of the time, 98.7 Kiss FM, New York during the early '80s was awash with great synthesizer records and a good fifty percent of them came from Prelude.

Formed at the height of the disco boom, Prelude had immediate success with Musique's In the Bush. Produced by Adams and mixed by Kevorkian, "In the Bush" was as bad lyrically as disco's detractors claimed, but its bungee bass-line was impossibly elastic, its keyboards heralded house music and the whole package was just about the most irresistible dance-floor track ever. On the other hand, the label's biggest American hit, France Joli's "Come to Me" (thankfully not included here), proved that Prelude was just as guilty of churning out dross as the bandwagon-jumping major labels.

Prelude's early releases were all more or less paint-by-numbers disco, but that changed with their last release of 1979, Inner Life's I'm Caught Up (In a One Night Love Affair). Produced by Adams and featuring vocals by the incomparable Jocelyn Brown, "I'm Caught Up"'s string-fuelled tale of the victim of a string of one-night stands became an enormous hit at Larry Levan's Paradise Garage, where it struck a chord with the hordes of hedonists who assembled there every weekend. "I'm Caught Up" was all gospel release and string melodrama, but Prelude also pursued a funkier direction.

Unlimited Touch's I Hear Music in the Streets was one of disco's innumerable odes to itself, but with its outrageously fat synth-bass riff that bordered on the sub-bass sound of hip-hop and drum'n'bass (especially on a big sound system) it looked ahead at the same time as it look inward. "I Hear Music in the Streets" was mostly the work of Bert Reid, who was probably the funkiest of Prelude's regular producers. He was also responsible for the wildly percussive mix of Secret Weapon's "Must Be the Music", which was another huge club hit in New York (and further proof of the proximity of disco and hip-hop in the early days not just with the rap, but with the percussion breaks that could have been lifted straight from Kool Herc's turntables). Perhaps even more rhythmic (and certainly weirder) was Rod Niangandoumou's surreal combination of Fela Kuti and rhinestone, Shake it Up (Do the Boogaloo).

"Shake it Up" was one of many examples of disco picking up on what would become known as world music. The most important of these was disco's use of Jamaican dub techniques to open up musical spaces and extend the flow motion so crucial to disco's aesthetic of the mix. One such stretched-out groove was Sharon Redd's Beat the Street, which (included here in its François Kevorkian mix) reached #41 on the US R&B chart (it was a Top 20 pop hit in Britain, however) pretty much on the strength of airplay and record sales in New York alone. With its dubby dynamics, an insistent synth that was like someone tugging your sleeve nonstop and drum programming that was so mechanical and frenetic that it resembled Piet Mondrian's painting, *Broadway Boogie Woogie*, set in motion, "Beat the Street" gave the lie to the naysayers who insisted that disco was nothing but a formulaic 4/4 beat.

⮐We almost chose **Absolutely . . .**
The Very Best of Prelude, Deep Beats, 1997